CHARLES SELIGER

CHARLES SELIGER

Ways of Nature

September 6 - October 25, 2008

Michael Rosenfeld Gallery
New York

We live in a wonderful world, and the wonders of the world without us are matched and more than matched by the wonders of the world within us. This interior world has its natural history also, and to observe and record any of its facts and incidents, or trace any of its natural processes, is well worthy of our best moments.

—John Burroughs from *Under the Apple Trees*, Volume XIX of the *Writings of John Burroughs*, 1916

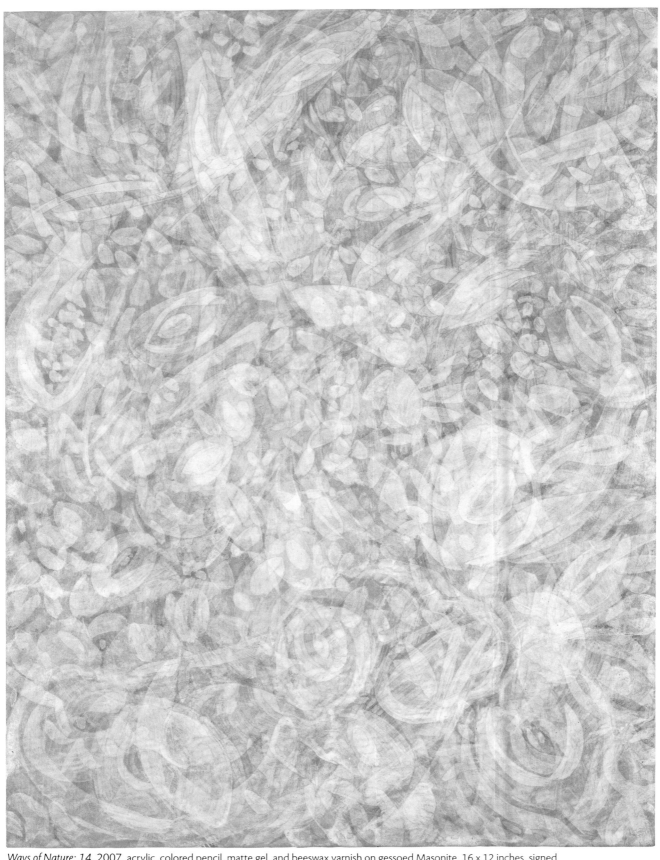

Ways of Nature: 14, 2007, acrylic, colored pencil, matte gel, and beeswax varnish on gessoed Masonite, 16 x 12 inches, signed

*I*t has been nearly sixty years since I discovered the nature writings of the American naturalist John Burroughs. His essays and poems evoke a sense of awe and contain a richly colored imagery that reflects his cherished and timeless world of organic nature with all its mysteries. In my painting, I have focused my imagination on the articulation of biomorphic imagery. "Ways of Nature" is the theme of this exhibition of new work and is the title of John Burroughs Vol XIV of the Riverby edition of his collected writings published by Houghton Mifflin.

— Charles Seliger, May 2008

Ways of Nature: 18, 2008, acrylic, Micron pen, colored pencil, matte gel, and beeswax varnish on gessoed Masonite, 10 x 8 inches, signed

*God has put a secret art into the forces of nature so as to enable it
to fashion itself out of chaos into a perfect world system.*[1]

"THE STRUCTURE OF BECOMING"—
CHARLES SELIGER'S EXPRESSIONS OF COMPLEXITY

by Michelle DuBois

*I*n 1943, Charles Seliger's paintings were exhibited for the first time at the Norlyst Gallery in New York. This year's *Ways of Nature* exhibition marks the sixty-fifth anniversary of Seliger's career as an artist and is therefore an appropriate moment to pause and consider that career, in both its historical and contemporary contexts. Though his career has intersected with numerous historical moments and stylistic fashions, his working methods, subject matter, and philosophy have remained remarkably consistent for over sixty years. Since the 1940s, Charles Seliger has been producing dense, small-scale, abstract paintings depicting his imaginary view of the complex spheres of nature that exist beyond or below human vision. An urbanite, Seliger's conceptions about nature are filtered through intellectual and poetic frameworks and are metaphysically, indeed, spiritually based. His paintings, consisting of an expressionist, painterly base finished with ultra-fine calligraphic markings, evoke the teeming realm of micro-organisms, cells and molecules, and the bodily viscera of humans, animals, and insects. His work simultaneously evokes the macrocosmic realm, dense with planets in the process of formation and destruction. Ultimately his paintings deal with the domain where all of these become the same.

The invisible elements of nature that Seliger depicts are in a perpetual state of change or metamorphosis. Borrowing a phrase from the philosopher Edmond Husserl, Seliger once described his paintings as portraying the "structure of becoming."[2] The dialectic embodied in this phrase perfectly summarizes Seliger's career-long quest to forge a reconciliation of opposites in his work. In each and every painting, he represents and enacts the struggle for control between chaos and order as it occurs in nature, and as it unfolds in the creative process he personally undergoes when creating a paint-

ing. Charles Seliger's paintings about what lies below or beyond the visible in nature are fundamentally about the nature of his own subjectivity and creative process.

The Production of a Painting: A Metaphor for Natural Processes

Influenced by the surrealists in exile in New York during World War II, Seliger has used automatism as a technique in the early phase of producing a painting for most of his career.[3] When he begins a work, he has no organizing principle, no direction or pre-meditated vision to his work. Seliger layers different colors of paint on the surface using big brushes, trowels, or paint knives, which he allows to dry between coats. His use of color is extraordinarily liberal and completely intuitive; sometimes the colors are associated with seasons, such as the wan gold of a field in winter or the green-yellow of new grass in spring. The riotous colors of the tropics—vivid orange, pink, aquamarine, and chartreuse—dominate some paintings. Deep, brooding blues and purples suggest the celestial realm and also ultraviolet light, impossible to see with the unaided human eye.

After applying layers of paint, Seliger then rubs, files, scrapes, and sands the paint away, reapplying more paint between sessions. This building up and removing (creative/destructive) phase takes months. The result is a dense, marbled surface as smooth as porcelain, with multiple layers of paint evident, sometimes adding up to a quarter-inch thick.[4] Seliger described how the creative process itself is metaphorical for him, stating, "In a way, I am bringing out an earlier history of the painting and an earlier memory or thought. My paintings are a form of excavation...like stones in the earth are a form of memory of the physical history of the earth."[5] In addition to the archaeological metaphor of excavation, Seliger also uses

---

1 Immanuel Kant, *Universal Natural History and the Theory of the Heavens,* trans. by S. Jaki (Edinburgh: Scottish Academic Press, 1981), 87.

2 In a December 1, 1980 journal entry, Seliger wrote: "I found a wonderful phrase while reading *Phenomenology and the Crisis of Philosophy* by Edmond Husserl, a phrase which I think states the nature of my painting in a most exact way: 'The Structure of Becoming,' two aspects of my work, so clear to me, in such a simple phrase. My paintings are always concerned with the most minute relationships and structure yet always remain in flux, in a state of becoming, never (in spite of the intensity and detail) to arrive at a final and recognizable form." Charles Seliger Journals, Collection of the Pierpont Morgan Library, Accession Number 6148, 1980.

3 Seliger's approach to art-making was particularly influenced by the younger English-speaking surrealists Roberto Matta and Gordon Onslow Ford, who used automatism in their endeavor to convey a state of being they called psychological morphology. Matta described it thus: "... to follow a form through a certain evolution. For instance, from a seed to a tree, the form is consistently changing under certain pressures until it arrives at its final

form and then disintegrates. Now, the growth in the change of a form, which concerns any organism, or even mineral — or — how should I say it — a stone which is exposed to accidents...this notion of morphology relates to how one's feelings were formed and transformed through life." Max Kozloff, "An Interview with Matta: 'These Things Were Like Rain Catching up with a Man who is Running.'" *Artforum*, September 1965, 23. Seliger read their essays in surrealist journals such as *View, VVV* and *London Bulletin*, journals he considers influential to his artistic development.

4 Because of this labor-intensive process, Seliger does not produce many paintings in any given year.

5 Seliger, interview with the author, June 20, 2007. Interestingly, in the 1940s, Seliger also began painting on stones and bones as an extension of his idea that stones are a form of earth's memory. These three-dimensional paintings are covered with dense, meticulous lines in rich colors.

the word "retrieval" to describe his artistic process.[6] By this he means that when he sands work down, he seeks to retrieve a passage in the earlier composition that has some significance to the current state of the work, thus, an earlier history or an earlier memory informs the identity of the current painting. Seliger's painting process is analogical to memory and concept formation in general. Just as he works on developing a usable surface by adding layers and continually going back to earlier layers, so too do we as individuals retrieve parts of history, personal or social, how and when we need to for current purposes.

Seliger continues this build-up and removal process until certain marks and forms seem to cohere in his mind into something that evokes an organic association. At this point, he consciously intervenes in the painting process. He uses all his knowledge, aesthetic techniques, and judgment about composition, color placement, and line to produce a painting that will convey his poetic, imaginative point of view about the natural forms that suggested themselves to him in patterns in the paint. Using micro-fine brushes, or perfectly sharpened colored pencils, he adds calligraphic markings: tiny, feathery lines, dots, swirls, and traces around colored passages, which suggest details of organisms, but which are not actually anything real or anything that coheres into something truly legible. In many of Seliger's paintings, this graphic quality is dominant. He begins a work in a painterly, expressionist, and uncontrolled manner, one requiring physical effort to later scrape and sand. Yet ultimately, because of the ultra-fine calligraphic markings, his finished paintings have a cerebral, disciplined, polished character. The nature that Seliger depicts begins in what seems to be a state of chaos, but the inchoate is ultimately revealed as reassuringly bound by order and inexorable, eternal laws.

The notion of an ordered universe implies a sense of divine purpose, a sense of the cosmic, or the spiritual (though of no creed and non-dogmatic). This characteristic of his work was noted as early as 1948, by his friend the poet Stanley Lawrence Berne who described Seliger's work in words applicable to this day:

> This art has a religious purpose. Its inspiration is the life-process... He chose... to follow the shape through the microscope until the object was forced to reveal its deep structure, the whole visceral foundation of life's ground-source. Now, the geology of the cell is made a fitting topic such that a reverence for life emerges and our excitement in a new 'art' experience pales before the re-establish-

ment of the fact that in a world of inevitable change-of-values, growth and birth proceed in an orderly pattern of improvement that has only existence and perfect function as its goal.[7]

Not only does Seliger deal with nature in a state of perpetual flux, but Seliger's very working style and technique can also be characterized as a state of constant metamorphosis and experimentation. He continuously works through formal issues and seeks again and again to enact this relationship between chaos and order, the unconscious and the conscious. To do so, he uses media as diverse as tempera, oil, acrylic, matte gel, charcoal, colored pencils, beeswax and a variety of varnishes. Seliger also employs an assortment of tools, especially to further his exploration of different properties of the line within his painting. He uses fine brushes, sometimes made from only a few hairs, the LeRoy pen (an architect's writing implement used to produce micro-fine lines on a blue-print) and tjanting device (another writing implement, used to make lines on batik fabrics). Each painting opens up a realm of inquiry for Seliger and sows the seeds for the next work. Rarely a day passes when Seliger does not paint or work on a painting.

Scale

Consistent with most of his work, the paintings in this exhibition are notably small in size. Seliger made his decision to produce very small paintings in the context of his earliest art milieu, the realm of the nascent abstract expressionist movement, of which he was considered a vital part.[8] From 1948 through 1950, many of the canonical abstract expressionists developed their signature styles. Pollock, de Kooning, Still, and Rothko (all of whom Seliger had been contextualized with in the previous five years), were making mural-sized paintings with aggressively physical, kinesthetic techniques such as flinging the paint, using wild, seemingly uncontrolled gestures, or soaking the canvases with broad bands of pure color to produce powerful color fields. During this same period, from 1948-50, Seliger chose to paint small and controlled work. For a few years, he produced a body of paintings which ranged in size from 10 ½ x 15 inches (the largest) to 4 x 6 inches (the smallest). While he did not paint this small on a consistent basis, it was frequent enough that from this point on, he was known as a painter of small works. His use of line also became meticulous at this time and was noted by critics (especially in the early 1950s) to be polished and well-crafted.[9] In an inter-

---

6 Seliger, interview with the author, June 20, 2007. Seliger sometimes feels a painting is not working for him and yet does not want to destroy the work. He stores such paintings in his attic for months, sometimes years. Periodically he reconsiders the work and if he sees passages where he can move forward, he brings them back into his studio to finish them. This is another form of actual, physical retrieval.

7 Stanley Lawrence Berne, untitled essay for exhibition brochure, *Charles Seliger, Recent Paintings and Drawings*, April 26-May 6, 1948, Carlebach Gallery, unpaginated. Artist's personal files, Mount Vernon, New York.

8 From 1943 until roughly 1950, Seliger figured prominently in the gallery scene and in the critical discourse about a new propensity in painting that came to be known as abstract expressionism. He was first recognized in 1943 by the artist/dealer Jimmy Ernst (son of Max Ernst) and had numerous exhibitions at Ernst's Norlyst Gallery (though Ernst was not actually his dealer). In 1945, Seliger was included in an important exhibition, *Personal Statement: A Painting Prophecy, 1950*, organized by David Porter, who sought

to introduce this cutting-edge art to Washington, D.C. and the rest of the country. Also in 1945, he was represented by the dealer Howard Putzel and included in his groundbreaking exhibition entitled *A Problem for Critics*, which is generally considered to be the first serious exhibition to seek to define abstract expressionism and articulate its European links. Artists in the show included Matta, Gorky, Gottlieb, Hofmann, Masson, Miró, Picasso, Pollock, Pousette-Dart, Seliger and Tamayo. After Putzel died in 1945, Seliger was represented by Peggy Guggenheim, whose Art of This Century gallery was an incubator of abstract expressionism. Seliger had a solo exhibition in 1945 at Art of This Century and was included in multiple group shows, as well as the *24th Venice Biennale* in 1948, which Guggenheim helped organize.

9 The *New York Times* critic Stuart Preston referred to him as a miniaturist, whose work is "...carefully pondered and painstakingly drawn." "New Year's Openings," the *New York Times*, January 7, 1951, 89. The critic at large for *Art Digest* referred to his "impeccable craftsmanship." Belle Krasne, "Reviews:

view, Seliger described that he found his peers' work lacking in discipline, too physical, too raw, and even violent in the cases of Pollock and de Kooning.[10] Seliger consciously staked out a position which was in relation to and yet in opposition to large-scale painting and raw, unfinished brushstrokes and the sort of relationship these engendered between painting and viewer. Seliger's technique of ultra-fine lines on small surfaces displayed a degree of control and finish that differed radically from the raw, painterly canvases of de Kooning, Pollock, and Motherwell. The level of sheer detail and the degree of concentration required to apprehend his small work stands in sharp contrast to the more monochromatic canvases that strike one in a gestalt, single-glance manner, such as the paintings of Rothko, Newman, and Gottlieb.

Though the work of his artistic peers is critical to consider when looking at his decision to paint small and intricate paintings, Seliger's choice to do so was not a contrarian position for its own sake. Just 22 when he chose this direction, Seliger was actively seeking to identify his unique strengths in order to build upon them. Small size was something he had always preferred, inspired by his long-standing admiration of Paul Klee and Mark Tobey.[11] The small physical sizes of his work, as well as the controlled, meticulous linear quality, were formal characteristics which contributed to the meaning of his paintings. First and foremost, the diminutive size was a logical formal means by which to convey his preferred subject matter, the invisible aspects of reality, that which is below the surface or beyond human vision.[12] One approaches his paintings at a close range as one would a microscope or a telescope, looking into his work in order to see other realms. The small physical format contributes literally to the meaning and experience of his work. Another function small size and gesture serves is that it puts into sharp contrast his artistic project of interrogating the interaction between the unconscious and conscious, chaos and order. His extraordinarily disciplined gesture reflects his conscious effort to impose control and order upon the swirling chaos that originally

welled up from his unconscious in the early automatist phase of producing a work. His careful gesture, applied upon a very small surface, magnifies the controlled and disciplined sensibility of his work relative to the uncontrolled, undisciplined, physical sensibility of a large Pollock or de Kooning painting.

Another function of small size in his painting is to forge an intimate relationship with the viewer. This intense drive to cultivate intimacy with the viewer was something Seliger shared with a number of his artistic peers in the 1940s and 1950s, including artists who worked on very large canvases.[13] The work by these artists is often described in terms of being powerful and aggressive, but certain evidence indicates that is not how they themselves saw their work. The idea of large size was to intensify the personal, emotional experience and connection between viewer and art, to make a maximum impact on the psychology of the viewer. These large paintings forge an intimacy by physically enveloping the viewer, enclosing, enfolding, engulfing the (smaller) viewer in a sort of embrace.

Seliger was very much driven by his desire to create an intimate encounter, but his concept of how to do this was different. Seliger preferred not to physically dominate his viewers. Instead, he sought an intimacy that was more cerebral and required viewers to make an effort, to work to understand his paintings. The small size entices a willing and interested spectator to draw physically near, to engage in close, careful, quiet contemplation. His small paintings with dense patterns require different modes of looking: gazing, scanning, and close reading.[14] The viewer's relationship with his work is a relationship that unfolds in time, in which one must slow down, pay attention, and make associations, follow lines of thought, follow digressions and tangents, and then step back and focus again on the whole. Seliger's work demands discipline to produce and also insists on a certain discipline from the viewer.

In several entries in his journals from the 1950s, Seliger describes his idea of the nature of the relationship he sought to generate between his paintings and their viewers, by com-

Charles Seliger" *Art Digest,* January 1, 1951, 16. This language is a sort of antithesis to that used to describe the abstract expressionist paintings.

10 Charles Seliger, interview with the author, August 9, 2006, Mount Vernon, New York. It should be noted that canonical abstract expressionists made many small paintings, but the larger works were best known and were seen as more definitive of this new art movement. For a discussion on this, see Jeffrey Wechsler, *Abstract Expressionism, Other Dimensions,* exh. cat. (New Brunswick, New Jersey: Jane Vorhees Zimmerli Art Museum, Rutgers University, 1989).

11 Charles Seliger, interview with the author, Mount Vernon, New York, December 4, 2006. He had not personally met Tobey when he made this work, though he was familiar with his art. They met in 1950 and remained close friends until Tobey passed away in 1975.

12 To visualize the invisible was a stated goal of Seliger's from at least 1945. For *A Painting Prophecy: 1950,* organized by David Porter in 1945, Seliger submitted the following statement: "I want to apostrophize micro-reality. I want to tear the skin from life, and, peering closely, to paint what I see. I want my brain to become a magnifying glass for the infinite minutiae of reality. Growth is the poetry of all art." Charles Seliger, "Personal Statement: Painting Prophecy, 1950," David Porter Papers, Archives of American Art, Smithsonian Institution, Reel N/70-27, Frame 383-392. Remarkably, Seliger has remained true to this artist's statement for over sixty years.

13 In a 1951 interview, Mark Rothko stated, "I paint very big pictures. I realize that historically the function of painting large pictures is something very grandiose and pompous. The reason why I paint them, however, is precisely because I want to be very intimate and human. To paint a small picture is to place yourself outside your experience, to look upon an

experience as a stereopticon view or a reducing glass. However you paint a larger picture, you are in it. It isn't something you command. " Mark Rothko, untitled statement, *Interiors,* no. 110 (May 1951), quoted in Caroline Jones, *Machine in the Studio: Constructing the Postwar American Artist* (Chicago: The University of Chicago Press, 1996), 50. In an interview with Thomas Hess, de Kooning, too, saw intimacy in his work, describing his Woman paintings as a quest for creating "intimate perceptions." Hess wrote, "He attempts to capture 'the feeling of familiarity you have when you look at somebody's big toe when close to it, or at a crease in a hand, or a nose or lips..." Hess, "De Kooning Paints a Picture," *Art News,* March 1953, 30. In 1958, Barnett Newman had himself photographed standing about a foot in front of his painting *Cathedra* to show the viewer's optimal location. He believed his work must be viewed at such close quarters so that it dominated both direct and peripheral vision. Standing so close, nothing else exists.

14 The small scale and calligraphic qualities of his paintings contributes to their functioning as books, causing just the sort of escape and absorption the prominent critic Clement Greenberg disliked. In his 1954 essay, "Abstraction and Representation," Greenberg described modern painting as eschewing the feeling of absorption that Seliger's painting generated. Greenberg wrote, "The picture has become an entity belonging to the same order of space as our bodies; it is no longer the vehicle of an imaginary equivalent of that order. Pictorial space has lost its 'inside' and become all 'outside.' The spectator can no longer escape into it from the space in which he himself stands." Greenberg, "Abstraction and Representation," *Art and Culture, Critical Essays* (Boston: Beacon Press, 1961), 136-137. Seliger's paintings function in a completely opposite manner.

paring the way his work functioned in comparison to that of Jackson Pollock. He articulated his concepts in several journal entries in 1957, in a response to an exhibition of Pollock's small watercolors at the Sidney Janis Gallery. The following entry is one of his most pointed on the subject:

> .... Janis's Pollock show, because of its [small] scale, comes off for me more than any of his other shows. Where the subjective elements are spread about in such enormous excess they lose their meaning and ability to communicate, whereas [sic] the smaller works express their emotion in a manner of being overheard – and therefore becomes more effective and revealing. The subjective is an intimate revelation – it is hard to be intimate on a billboard. So many of the Abstract Expressionists [sic] seem to have emotions which sustain only one simple emotion – a static reiteration of one constant feeling or mood is hardly a revelation of the inner, moving, living emotional life of a man.[15]

This journal entry is illuminating for what it reveals about Seliger's notion of the intimate. The relationship between his small paintings and the viewer is less physical and more cognitive and empathetic; intimacy develops as a viewer seeks to understand an artwork's complexities and nuances and follow Seliger's train of thought. The "inner, moving, living emotional life" is ultimately what his paintings are about.

Implicit too in Seliger's small paintings executed in the context of the enormous, mural sized paintings of the late 1940s and 1950s, is his preoccupation with scale as a relative concept, as opposed to just size for its own sake. Size as a concept is a fairly straightforward matter of measurements; however, the issue of scale is complex and more nuanced. Scale is a relative term: bigness needs smallness to function as such and vice versa. Size is a physical characteristic and physically positions us as a viewer, while scale induces multiple other complicated associations, usually on a more philosophical level. Scale is something that can be related to size but usually transcends the actual painting and requires a different type of work from the viewer. One of the earliest scholars of abstract expressionism, William Seitz wrote, "Scale does not exist without structure...It implies a measure: Is it man, nature, the machine, the immaterial absolute? ...If the idea of scale is to be fully useful as a key to the richest meanings of the arts, it must be further enlarged: it must encompass more than the material and the perceptual...One must consider its philosophical scale."[16] Scale refers to a concept of relativity between viewer and painting and then beyond. Scale implies relationships with

nature and more spectacularly, with the infinite, or the immaterial absolute as Seitz eloquently described it. The content of Seliger's painting—nature—is elusive, implied, sensed, but not manifest. His paintings refer to worlds within worlds and make us feel simultaneously dominant (because of our larger size) and yet, paradoxically, also on the verge of being pulled into a vortex and losing ourselves. The concepts of relativity and flow of matter are activated by his paintings.

Seliger's paintings ultimately require a less physical, more cerebral relationship to both viewers and nature. Produced in the context when his peers made large paintings, Seliger's small paintings are related to and engage in a dialogue with their work.[17] His decision to paint small when many preferred large paintings was complicated and based on a number of personal and professional factors. However, it was distinctly calculated as a response to and a sort of negation of the large canvasses and the associated rhetoric of the heroic, the dominant, and the masculine that surrounded this work.

Metaphysical Abstraction

Seliger's decision to make very small, very refined paintings in the late 1940s became a pivotal one for his career, and it was at this point where comparisons between him and the abstract expressionists start to wane. In 1950, Marian Willard, owner of the Williard Gallery, took Seliger on as one part of her stable of artists,[18] and beginning that year, Seliger's work was more frequently compared to that of other artists affiliated with the gallery, including Mark Tobey, Morris Graves, Lee Mullican, and Norman Lewis. Seliger's social and artistic association with artists at the Willard Gallery and especially the contextualization of his work with Mark Tobey shaped the reception of his work for decades. Like Seliger, these artists all have a vexed relationship with abstract expressionism; their work is related to it, but in an uneasy way. While scholars and dealers often argue that these artists were accidentally or willfully omitted from the canon, instead of seeking to revise the canon, another productive approach would be to look at Seliger (and certain other abstract painters at this time) as representing a separate, though related, sensibility.[19] Seliger and his peers at the Willard Gallery were producing something vital, important, and distinct, related to abstract expressionism as a quiet, controlled, more linear counterpoint. Usually working on a smaller scale, these artists tended to paint abstractly in a fine, linear, and calligraphic manner; and their work was muted and "quiet" in appearance compared to the canonical abstract expressionists. Seliger and as a number of Willard's artists, were notable for

15 Journal Entry, November 29, 1957, Charles Seliger Journals, Collection of the Pierpont Morgan Library, New York, Accession Number 6148, 1957.

16 William Seitz, *Abstract Expressionist Painting in America* (Cambridge: Harvard University Press and the National Gallery of Art, Washington 1983), 84.

17 When asked in an interview about his decision to paint such small works, Seliger stated, "There was all this stuff going on about scale and my gift was the ability to deal with small scale in a highly complex way, in a manner in which large would not be the same." Charles Seliger, interview with the author, Mount Vernon, New York, January 9, 2008.

18 According to Marian Willard, when Peggy Guggenheim closed her gallery in 1947, Guggenheim personally asked her to represent Jackson Pollock and Charles Seliger. Willard, who had represented Mark Tobey for several years by this time, declined to take on Pollock, stating she felt strongly that

she could not represent both Tobey and Pollock. Though they had many intriguing similarities and were both "giants" in her words, ultimately they were too different, even opposed to each other in approaches. Pollock went with Betty Parsons. Of all of Guggenheim's artists, Marian Willard took on only Seliger, whose work she believed had a similar sensibility to other artists in her gallery. Marian Willard, interview by Paul Cummings, June 3, 1969, transcript, the Archives of American Art, 26.

19 In Seliger's journals from the 1950s, he often laments the lack of critical attention he and his peers at the Willard are receiving, but nowhere in his writing does he state that he believed he was an overlooked abstract expressionist. He describes extensive conversations with his peers at the Willard Gallery, and the nature of their complaint was about the monocular vision of contemporary critics, who concentrated on only one group and downplayed or ignored others. As Seliger once put it, "We all get

the very fine lines in their paintings, which were often referred to as calligraphic in the Asian sense, where the line incorporates both draftsmanship and creative gesture. Another distinctive quality to their work is that it was often seen as "spiritual," "mystical," and "metaphysical," all labels applied to Willard Gallery artists.[20]

There are also numerous examples of critics in the 1950s and 1960s discussing the Willard Gallery as possessing a distinct sensibility such as having a "twilight mood" or being "muted." While it is not always the case that considering a dealer and the artists of a particular gallery as a group will shed light on aspects of the artists' work, in the case of the Willard Gallery, significant elements of Marian Willard's philosophy about the role and function of art should be considered when looking at not only Seliger's work as he matured as an artist, but also the reception of his work throughout a large swath of his career. She had a certain philosophical lens shaped by Jungian theories through which she evaluated paintings and selected artists to represent. Willard had attended Jung's lectures weekly while living in Zurich in 1937 and thus was well-educated in his philosophy; she believed the artists whose work she represented referred in some way to a way to a universal, collective unconscious.[21] Influenced by Jung's ideas about art and the spiritual as well as by the Eastern philosophies that informed Jung, Willard ascribed to art a lofty purpose:

> We've got to reorient ourselves to our own unconscious and sort of begin again from the beginning. We can't look to any higher force to do it for us anymore. Art was once portraying religion. Then it went into, if you want to say, Surrealism and the unconscious, the subjective. But both were quite different from what I was feeling and hoping. I think what people are looking for is something that they can, in a personal way, orient themselves to the universal [sic] Creative people have to do it. Most people get away without doing it.[22]

Seliger's approach to nature prior to 1950 was to focus on a primordial realm of cells, fossils, geology, and primitive, single-celled creatures. During his time at the Willard Gallery, Seliger's focus shifted away from more the concrete aspects of nature towards more abstract ideas: states of nature such as energy, light, and movement; conceptions of the past and future; and questions concerning the nature of time, leading a critic for the *New York Times* to call his work "metaphysical abstraction."[23] His work became more preoccupied with ideas about nature where theoretical science and spirituality converge, and it has remained thus ever since.

Charles Seliger and Mark Tobey

Seliger's "metaphysical abstraction" was developed in the context of the Willard Gallery, but Seliger in particular honed his ideas through long discussions and correspondence with the painter Mark Tobey. One of Charles Seliger's most intimate and enduring personal friendships and artistic companionships was with Tobey, whom he met in 1950 and remained close with until Tobey's death in 1975.[24] Since Mark Tobey was thirty-six years older than Seliger, it is often assumed that Tobey was the mentor and Seliger the protégé; however, reading their correspondence and Seliger's journal entries, it becomes apparent that the relationship was mutually influential and supportive. Seliger gave Tobey advice and opinions on his art nearly as much as Tobey advised on Seliger's art.

There are many similarities between the two artists in both their painting styles and their philosophies. Both artists preferred to work on a small scale (though in the 1960s, Tobey began making larger paintings), and both produced paintings with dense, fine, linear components, which convey notions of immensity and universality. Seliger's paintings in the 1950s and 1960s were far more linear than they are now. Critics in the 1950s and 1960s routinely compared Seliger's paintings to Tobey's and sometimes even mistook Seliger's work for Tobey's. The two artists also had similar philosophical views about nature and humanity that they wished to communicate

shelved while the A.E. boys have their day. They win by...quantity not quality, 'the mostest with the muchest." Journal Entry, March 3, 1956, *Charles Seliger Journals*, Collection of Pierpont Morgan Library, Accession No. 6148, 1956. (Here, he was discussing a conversation he had with Norman Lewis while they visited the Whitney Museum.)

20 In certain correspondence, as well as in articles written by Willard, she seems to be trying to distinguish her artists on this spiritual basis and also to differentiate them from the abstract expressionists. There are multiple examples of this, but to give just one: in a letter to Morris Graves, she wrote, "After fifteen years of searching for spiritual content in painting and becoming known for it-even if I have been called a 'Sunday School' - the people who are also searching for it are coming to me. We are still a small group but I have daily proof that the seed is growing and that an increasing number of the public is aware of it....My trip to Europe served to reinforce this determination as I found nothing there that seemed to be going in this direction. They are adept in technique and slick in salesmanship, but not in searching...most of 57th Street turns toward them; I turn away and in so doing turn to the East for synthesis and Zen to steady our search for our own expressions of universal truths." Marian Willard, letter to Morris Graves, November 12, 1952, reprinted in Ray Kass, *Morris Graves, Vision of the Inner Eye* (Washington, D.C.: George Braziller and the Phillips Collection, 1983), 59.

21 Willard was also interested in Asian art and had several Japanese artists in her stable of artists in the 1950s. There are many well-documented studies on how Jung's theory of the collective unconscious was indebted to Asian religions. In his writings, Jung refers to traditions as diverse as Hinduism, Indian Buddhism, Tibetan Buddhism, Japanese Buddhism, and Chinese Taoism, interpreting "Eastern" thought as a blend of philosophy and psychology, and borrowing heavily from Asian traditions to formulate his concepts of personality types and the synthesizing of opposites. His theory of the collective unconscious in particular was heavily influenced by Taoism. For more on Jung's indebtedness to Asian philosophies in general, see Harold Coward, *Jung and Eastern Thought* (Albany: State University of New York Press, 1985);on his indebtedness to Taoism, see Coward, "Taoism and Jung: Synchronicity and the Self," in *Philosophy East & West*, Volume 46, Number 4, October, 1996, pp 477-496.

22 Marian Willard, interview with Cummings, 19.

23 Stuart Preston of the *New York Times* wrote that Seliger used "expressive draftsmanship for its own sake...Animals and growing things are his nominal subjects, but he goes deep into their heart, painting what might be their ghosts...This is metaphysical abstraction, catching some semblance of a likeness in the network of line. Seliger is a refined and devious draftsman, using the brush like a pen. "Modern Variety, Synchromy, Calligraphy and Suggestion," the *New York Times*, February 20, 1955, X13.

24 In discussing artists in her gallery, Willard noted that Tobey and Seliger were "...great pals...They go off on trips together and visit Feininger...the must have been just about twenty years apart, probably more, but they had quite a relationship, got stimulation from each other." Willard, interview with Cummings, 47. The two of them were among those who had the largest number of one-man shows at the Willard Gallery: Seliger had nine one-man shows and Tobey fourteen. (From a list of Willard Gallery exhibitions compiled from her personal papers by Miani Johnson, Marian Willard's daughter.) Other artists who were shown about the same number of times as Seliger were the sculptor David Smith and Genichuro Inokuma.

in their paintings. As discussed, Seliger's artistic project—developed at a young age and honed and deepened over decades—deals fundamentally with the process of morphology and the interconnectedness of all of nature, including our position to and relationship within it. Seliger's large and ambitious aim is to convey the essence of the evolution of us all: from the smallest cells, towards greater complexity, birth, maturity, death, and dispersal back into the atmosphere, to regenerate again into something new. This metaphysics was something he shared with Mark Tobey, though Tobey's work was often discussed in terms of his Baha'i faith and its fundamental notions of unity, progressive revelation, and humanity. There is a strong emphasis on universality and oneness of all in this religion, which was a world-view Tobey sought to convey in his work.[25] Tobey also sought to depict nature, and in his work he depicted it as having the same energy and essence as a metropolis. Tobey, like Seliger, was interested in showing the complex relationships of all beings and states of being, a fundamentally spiritual endeavor.

Seliger in the Contemporary Art Realm: Complexity, Density, Small-Scale

Seliger's decades-long artistic project of picturing the structure of becoming and dealing with a realm beyond or below human vision converges intriguingly with some facets of contemporary thought and contemporary painting, namely the influence of complexity theory, which addresses the complexity of scientific, social, and even artistic systems.[26] An avid reader, when Seliger became aware of this theory in the 1990s, he was thrilled to find he was in the company of a number of other like-minded thinkers in science, computer science, economics, as well as in the arts who were interested in how order arrives out of what seems like chaos. The basis of complexity theory is a rejection of the "reductionist" notion in science and modernism that everything be broken down to its smallest and simplest components. Instead, those who believe in complexity theory look at systems, analyzing how minute particles, bits of information, or large groups of people cohere into ordered systems.

The idea that complexity, rather than simplification, is a framework for understanding our contemporary state of being has been around since at least the turn of the twentieth century, but the computer has greatly aided the study of complexity by enabling the processing of vast amounts of data in order to compare patterns. One of Seliger's favorite books on the subject is *Frontiers of Complexity, The Search for Order in a Chaotic World* in which the authors describe complexity thus:

> Within science, complexity is a watchword for a new way of thinking about the collective behavior of many basic but interacting units, be they atoms, molecules, neurons, or bits within a computer... complexity is the study of the behavior of macroscopic collections of such units that are endowed with the potential to evolve in time. Their interactions lead to coherent collective phenomena, so-called emergent properties that can be described only at higher levels than those of the individual units....the whole is more than the sum of its components, just as a Van Gogh is so much more than a collection of bold brushstrokes.[27]

The tendency towards complexity in the arts was first observed in the realm of music, in a movement labeled "new complexity" in the 1980s, especially in Great Britain. New complexity composers such as James Clark, Brian Feeneyhough, and Richard Toop wrote music that was full of detail, precision, and intricacy and through these formal means, sought to convey complicated situations—for example, the human brain when filled with different thoughts in reaction to a difficult situation or a large city, where an enormous number of events take place simultaneously.[28]

Certain contemporary artists deal with this multi-valent concept of complexity and the multiplicity of systems of thought that inform and dictate our existence, in the digital age in particular. Some of the best known practitioners of this sort of painting were included in a recent Whitney exhibition titled *Remote Viewing: Invented Worlds in Recent Painting and Drawing*.[29] Seliger's art corresponds especially well to certain artists in this show, particularly Julie Mehretu, who layers her paintings with vast quantities of visual information culled from newspapers, maps, the Internet, architectural plans, and more. Her paintings are constructed worlds filled with data and information which never quite cohere into something recognizable. Her paintings require time to read and digest. This temporal element incorporated into dense abstract painting also defines the work of Matthew Ritchie, whose work contains layers of data from such diverse sources as the field of quantum physics to religious texts and tenets. He has said of his work, "I know it's hard to accept that the world is as complicated as it appears to be. But in the end we only have two

25 William Seitz, *Mark Tobey* (New York: The Museum of Modern Art and Doubleday and Co., 1962), 10. Seliger was not a member of the B'Hai faith, though they shared similar sentiments about the interconnectedness of all beings.

26 I certainly would not seek to define an over-arching sensibility or discover an essential quality to contemporary paintings. Also, to describe Seliger's work in the contemporary context is not to say younger artists were necessarily influenced by Seliger's work or he by theirs. Rather, a number of artists are pursuing the same lines of inquiry.

27 Peter Coveney and Roger Highfield, *Frontiers of Complexity: The Search for Order in a Chaotic World* (New York: Fawcett Columbine, 1995), 7. Seliger's other favorite books on the subject of complexity include: M. Mitchell Waldrop, *Complexity: The Emerging Science at the Edge of Order and Chaos* (New York: Simon and Schuster) 1992; Murray Gell-Man, *The Quark and the Jaguar: Adventures in the Simple and the Complex* (New York: MacMillan Press, 1995); and Matthieu Ricard and Trinh Yuan Thuan, *The Quantum and the Lotus* (New York: Random House, 2004).

28 I am indebted to David Ryan for generating this area of inquiry for me. Ryan was seeking to articulate some prominent strands in contemporary painting, and noticing a tendency towards complicated, dense thinking wrote, "The issue of this 'new complexity'- to borrow a term from contemporary music-actually forms a thread that might bind these artists together in a loose way. The emphasis is also on the complex legacy of American abstraction as both a 'negative' catalyst and an ongoing source of reference." David Ryan, *Talking Painting: Dialogues With Twelve Contemporary Abstract Painters* (New York: Routledge, 2002), viii. New complexity and the idea of American mid-century abstraction as a negative catalyst could both certainly apply to Seliger's paintings, though he was not included in this study.

29 In an essay for the catalogue, Katy Siegel wrote "No single quality binds these artists together, but each shares some theme or practice with several others, so that we might locate them in interconnected constellations... these commonalities include intense drawing, obsessive studio practices,

options: either embrace complexity and the freedom that comes with it, or hide behind the veil of appearance and prejudice."[30] Steve DiBenedetto also deals with complexity and multiple levels of reality in his paintings, which have been described as "topsy-turvy underworlds that disturb almost as much as they enchant...swirls, lattices and vortices crisscross, interweave, sever and re-form, resulting in a kaleidoscopic vision a of deep unconscious in apparent distress."[31]

Other artists who share Seliger's interest in complexity as well as his practice of producing small paintings include James Siena and Thomas Nozkowski, artists whom Seliger knows and whose work he admires. James Siena makes very small, patterned paintings, dense with contiguous, undulating lines that seem to breathe or vibrate with energy. Siena's paintings have been described as the visual equivalent to the field of artificial intelligence—the effort to produce a computer that not only has intelligent functioning but also the capacity to be reflective and understand itself (a subject of great interest to complexity theorists). Siena deals with patterns and systems of thought. Thomas Nozkowski likewise works on a small scale and addresses knowledge and experience, but of a personal kind, choosing to engage only with topics he has experienced, seen, read, or heard first-hand. Like Seliger, Nozkowski also layers and wipes down his paintings repeatedly, creating rich, dense layers that serve as metaphors for memory and time.

In our computer-screen dominated age, technology has perhaps finally produced the perfect viewer for a Seliger painting by training us to patiently scan small surfaces for minute graphic markings and visual motifs. In an era where technology gets ever smaller, slimmer, and more refined, Seliger's small, meticulous paintings are in some ways better suited for a contemporary viewer than a mid-century viewer, when largeness was prized in all arenas.

Conclusion

Seliger's sensibility, though grounded in modernism and mid-century abstraction, was in many ways a counterpoint to abstract expressionism—individualized, differentiated and yet fundamentally related to it. Seliger produced paintings that were about his subjectivity, referred to the universal and courted an intimate encounter with the viewer. Yet he sought to do this by making small paintings, dense with layers of paint and refined lines. Seliger has long held the belief that modernity is marked by ever greater categorization, discoveries of ever smaller particles and smaller forms of energy. The more we as humans discover, the more complex, instead of simple, our reality becomes, and it can seem that we are verging on chaos. The interface between chaos and order has intrigued Seliger personally and intellectually for decades, as a relationship that occurs on every level of the cosmos: in a cell, in one's psyche, in his own creative process, and in the celestial realm. As one of the better-known authors on complexity theory described:

> All complex systems have somehow acquired the ability to bring order and chaos into a special kind of balance. The balance point-often called the edge of chaos – is where the components of a system never quite lock into place and yet never dissolve into turbulence, either. The edge of chaos is where life has enough stability to sustain itself and enough creativity to deserve the name life. The edge of chaos is where new ideas and innovative genotypes are forever nibbling away at the edges of the status quo, and where the entrenched old guard will eventually be overthrown.[32]

Seliger's paintings dealing with the complexity of nature in its scientific and spiritual realms are inherently generative, fecund with possibilities for further exploration and discovery. His paintings about the "structure of becoming" deal fundamentally with complexity and the process of regeneration, and they are ultimately optimistic statements about the future.

Michelle DuBois is a doctoral candidate in art history at Boston University with an emphasis on American modern and contemporary art. She is a co-author of the catalogue raisonné on Jacob Lawrence and the managing editor of the accompanying monograph, *Jacob Lawrence: Over the Line,* awarded the George Wittenborn Award for Excellence in Art Publications in 2000. DuBois has been a Benjamin Rowland Fellow and a Jacob Rosenberg Fellow in the Department of American Painting, Sculpture and Decorative Arts at the Harvard Art Museums. She is the recipient of the Henry Luce Foundation American Art Dissertation Award (awarded by Boston University) and the Bease and Harry Adelson Travel Grant Award for American Art Dissertation Research. Her dissertation, *Picturing "The Structure of Becoming" – Charles Seliger's Complex Expressionism*, will be completed at the end of 2008.

expressionist passages, personal cosmologies and iconographies, the desire to model a world within a painting, irrational space, outer space and other fantastic imagery, multiple perspectives, a wondrous attitude towards science...in addition, the paintings all directly and obliquely address possible relationships between the exterior, material world and the interior, sensing self." *Remote Viewing: Invented Worlds in Recent Painting and Drawing*, exh. cat. (New York: Whitney Museum of American Art in association with Harry N. Abrams, 2005), 96.

30 Elizabeth Grady, "Matthew Richie," *Remote Viewing*, 58.

31 Tina Kukielski, "Steve DiBenedetto," *Remote Viewing*, 27. DiBenedetto has stated that his ultimate goal is to give us "...a greater sense of place in the big picture," 30.

32 M. Mitchell Waldrop, *Complexity: The Emerging Science at the Edge of Order and Chaos* (New York: Simon and Schuster, 1992), 12.

A Selection of Paintings
2006 – 2008

Ways of Nature: 1, 2006, acrylic, colored pencil, matte gel, and beeswax varnish on gessoed Masonite, 12 x 16 inches, signed

Ways of Nature: 2, 2006, acrylic, colored pencil, matte gel, and beeswax varnish on gessoed Masonite, 12 x 12 inches, signed

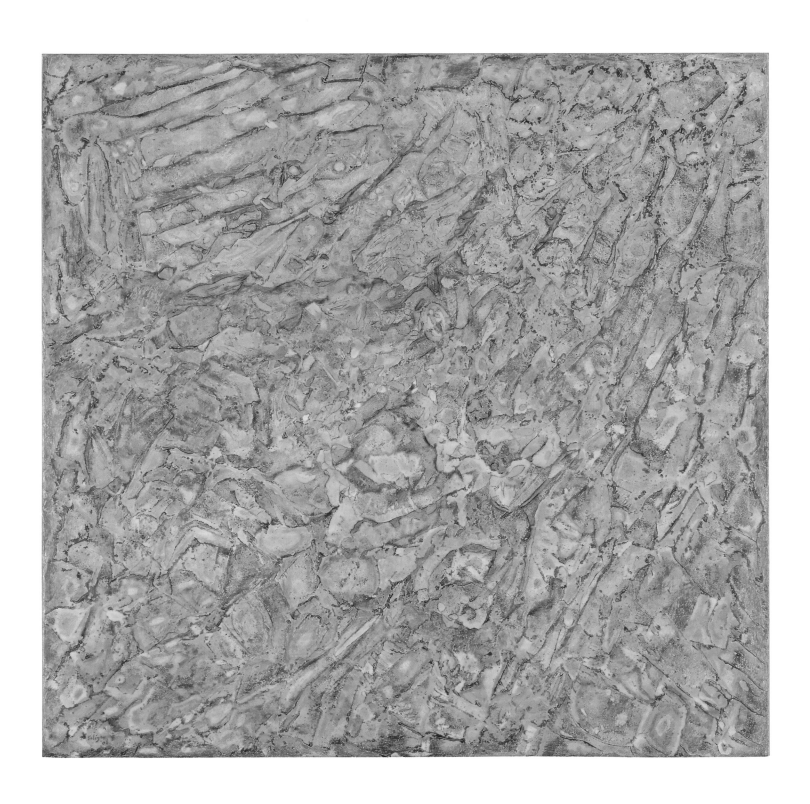

Ways of Nature: 3, 2006, acrylic, colored pencil, matte gel, and beeswax varnish on gessoed Masonite, 12 x 12 inches, signed

Ways of Nature: 4, 2007, acrylic, colored pencil, matte gel, and beeswax varnish on gessoed Masonite, 12 x 12 inches, signed

Ways of Nature: 5, 2007, acrylic, colored pencil, matte gel, and beeswax varnish on gessoed Masonite, 12 x 12 inches, signed

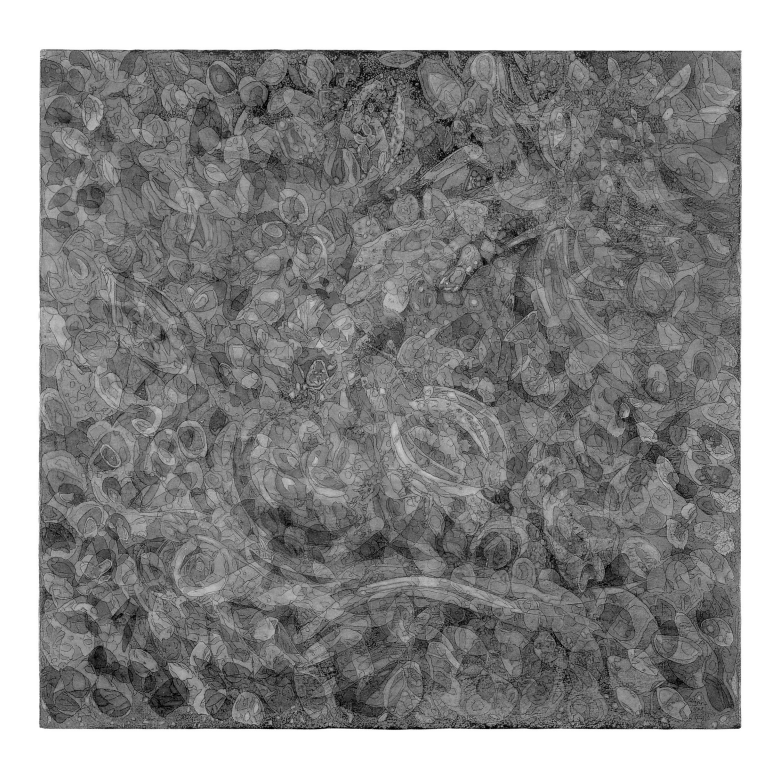

Ways of Nature: 6, 2007, acrylic, colored pencil, matte gel, and beeswax varnish on gessoed Masonite, 12 x 12 inches, signed

Ways of Nature: 7, 2007, acrylic, colored pencil, matte gel, and beeswax varnish on gessoed Masonite, 14 x 11 inches, signed

Ways of Nature: 8, 2007, acrylic, colored pencil, matte gel, and beeswax varnish on gessoed Masonite, 16 x 12 inches, signed

Ways of Nature: 9, 2007, acrylic, colored pencil, matte gel, and beeswax varnish on gessoed Masonite, 16 x 20 inches, signed

Ways of Nature: 10, 2007, acrylic, colored pencil, matte gel, and beeswax varnish on gessoed Masonite, 16 x 20 inches, signed

Ways of Nature: 11, 2007, acrylic, colored pencil, matte gel, and beeswax varnish on gessoed Masonite, 24 x 12 inches, signed

Ways of Nature: 12, 2007, acrylic, colored pencil, matte gel, and beeswax varnish on gessoed Masonite, 18 x 14 inches, signed

Ways of Nature: 13, 2007, acrylic, colored pencil, matte gel, and beeswax varnish on gessoed Masonite, 12 x 24 inches, signed

Ways of Nature: 15, 2008, acrylic, matte gel, and beeswax varnish on gessoed Masonite, 16 x 20 inches, signed

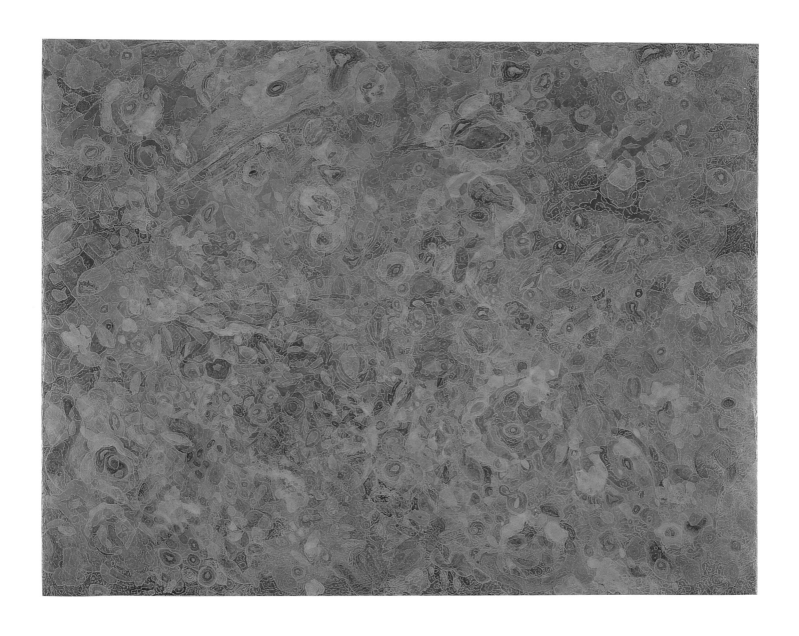

Ways of Nature: 16, 2008, acrylic, colored pencil, matte gel, and beeswax varnish on gessoed Masonite, 12 x 24 inches, signed

Ways of Nature: 17, 2008, acrylic, Micron pen, colored pencil, matte gel, and beeswax varnish on gessoed Masonite, 16 x 20 inches, signed

Ways of Nature: 19, 2008, acrylic, colored pencil, matte gel, and beeswax varnish on gessoed Masonite, 18 x 14 inches, signed

CHARLES SELIGER

EXHIBITION CHECKLIST

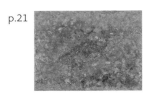

p.21

Ways of Nature: 1, 2006
acrylic, colored pencil,
matte gel, and beeswax varnish
on gessoed Masonite
12 x 16 inches, signed

p.31

Ways of Nature: 6, 2007
acrylic, colored pencil,
matte gel, and beeswax varnish
on gessoed Masonite
12 x 12 inches, signed

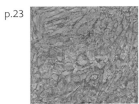

p.23

Ways of Nature: 2, 2006
acrylic, colored pencil,
matte gel, and beeswax varnish
on gessoed Masonite
12 x 12 inches, signed

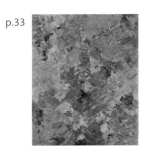

p.33

Ways of Nature: 7, 2007
acrylic, colored pencil,
matte gel, and beeswax
varnish on gessoed Masonite
14 x 11 inches, signed

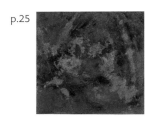

p.25

Ways of Nature: 3, 2006
acrylic, colored pencil,
matte gel, and beeswax
varnish on gessoed Masonite
12 x 12 inches, signed

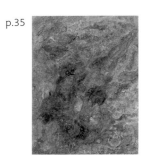

p.35

Ways of Nature: 8, 2007
acrylic, colored pencil,
matte gel, and beeswax varnish
on gessoed Masonite
16 x 12 inches, signed

p.27

Ways of Nature: 4, 2007
acrylic, colored pencil,
matte gel, and beeswax varnish
on gessoed Masonite
12 x 12 inches, signed

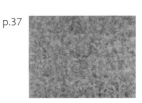

p.37

Ways of Nature: 9, 2007
acrylic, colored pencil,
matte gel, and beeswax varnish
on gessoed Masonite
16 x 20 inches, signed

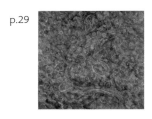

p.29

Ways of Nature: 5, 2007
 acrylic, colored pencil,
matte gel, and beeswax varnish
on gessoed Masonite
12 x 12 inches, signed

p.39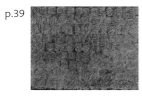

Ways of Nature: 10, 2007
acrylic, colored pencil,
matte gel, and beeswax
varnish on gessoed Masonite
16 x 20 inches, signed

p.47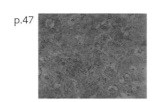

Ways of Nature: 15, 2008
acrylic, matte gel, and beeswax
varnish on gessoed Masonite
16 x 20 inches, signed

p.41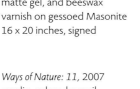

Ways of Nature: 11, 2007
acrylic, colored pencil,
 matte gel, and beeswax
varnish on gessoed Masonite
24 x 12 inches, signed

p.49

Ways of Nature: 16, 2008
acrylic, colored pencil,
matte gel, and beeswax
varnish on gessoed Masonite
12 x 24 inches, signed

p.51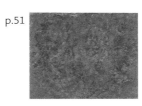

Ways of Nature: 17, 2008
acrylic, Micron pen, colored
pencil, matte gel, and beeswax
varnish on gessoed Masonite
16 x 20 inches, signed

p.43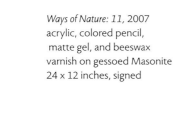

Ways of Nature: 12, 2007
acrylic, colored pencil,
matte gel, and beeswax
varnish on gessoed Masonite
18 x 14 inches, signed

p.10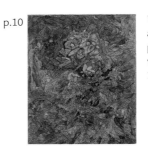

Ways of Nature: 18, 2008
acrylic, Micron pen, colored
pencil, matte gel, and beeswax
varnish on gessoed Masonite
10 x 8 inches, signed

p.45

Ways of Nature: 13, 2007
acrylic, colored pencil,
matte gel, and beeswax
varnish on gessoed Masonite,
12 x 24 inches, signed

p.8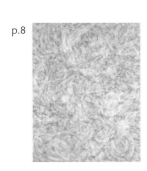

Ways of Nature: 14, 2007
acrylic, colored pencil,
matte gel, and beeswax
varnish on gessoed Masonite
16 x 12 inches, signed

p.53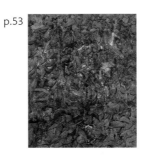

Ways of Nature: 19, 2008
acrylic, colored pencil,
matte gel and beeswax
varnish on gessoed Masonite
18 x 14 inches, signed

*M*ichael Rosenfeld Gallery has represented Charles Seliger for eighteen years. Since 1990, the gallery has mounted nine solo exhibitions and published seven catalogues presenting scholarly essays by art historians Isabelle Dervaux, Sam Hunter, Gail Levin, Addison Parks, John Yau, and most recently, Michelle DuBois, who is completing the first doctoral dissertation on Seliger's art and career. Contributors to catalogues have also included artist James Sienna and Nobel Prize recipient Roald Hoffmann. In 2002, Hudson Hills published *Charles Seliger: Redefining Abstract Expressionism* by Francis V. O'Connor, with a preface by Thomas M. Messer and an introduction by Melvin P. Lader. This monograph, the first devoted to Seliger, offered a rare glimpse at the working methods and personal life of an artist who, in his life-long pursuit of organic abstraction, contributed to the rise of abstract expressionism. The following year, Seliger received the Lee Krasner Award from the Pollock-Krasner Foundation in recognition of his long and illustrious artistic career. In 2005, the Morgan Library & Museum acquired the 148 hand-written volumes that comprise the artist's journals. Beginning in 1952 and spanning nearly sixty years, they contain Seliger's careful meditations on a wide range of topics, and they offer invaluable insights into some of the most dynamic decades in the history of art from the viewpoint of one of its most perceptive participants.

Influenced early on by the surrealist technique of automatism, Seliger has cultivated an eloquent and poetic style of abstraction that explores the dynamics of order and chaos animating the celestial, geographical, and biological realms. Today, he is best known for his meticulously detailed, small-scale paintings that function as both abstract works and intricate representations of the microscopic universes that exist in the natural world. Seliger has also earned a reputation as an innovator of artistic techniques, having developed his own methods for covering, scraping, and marking the surfaces of Masonite and canvas. A master craftsman who paints fewer than ten paintings a year, Seliger has influenced numerous generations of artists. It is a privilege and honor to represent Charles Seliger, and Michael Rosenfeld Gallery remains devoted to the vitality and future of his art.

CHARLES SELIGER

(American, b.1926)

SELECTED MUSEUM COLLECTIONS

Addison Gallery of American Art, Phillips Academy, Andover, MA
Arkansas Arts Center, Little Rock, AR
Art Institute of Chicago, Chicago, IL
Avampato Discovery Museum, Charleston, WV
Baltimore Museum of Art, Baltimore, MD
The British Museum, London, England
Brooklyn Museum of Art, Brooklyn, NY
Carnegie Museum of Art, Pittsburgh, PA
Greenville County Museum of Art, Greenville, SC
Herbert F. Johnson Museum, Cornell University, Ithaca, NY
High Museum of Art, Atlanta, GA
Hirshhorn Museum and Sculpture Garden, Washington, DC
The Israel Museum, Jerusalem, Israel
Jacksonville Art Museum, Jacksonville, FL
Jane Voorhees Zimmerli Art Museum, Rutgers University,
    New Brunswick, NJ
Long Beach Museum of Art, Long Beach, CA
Mead Art Museum, Amherst College, Amherst, MA
The Metropolitan Museum of Art, New York, NY
Milwaukee Art Museum, Milwaukee, WI
The Mint Museum of Art, Charlotte, NC
Mississippi Museum of Art, Jackson, MS
Mobile Museum of Art, Mobile, AL
The Morgan Library and Museum, New York, NY
Municipal Art Museum, The Hague, Holland
Munson-Williams-Proctor Institute, Utica, NY
The Museum of Fine Arts, Houston, TX
Museum of Modern Art, New York, NY
Neuberger Museum of Art, Purchase College, State College of
    New York, Purchase, NY
The Newark Museum, Newark, NJ
New Orleans Museum of Art, New Orleans, LA
The New York Public Library, New York, NY
Norton Museum of Art, West Palm Beach, FL
Ogunquit Museum of American Art, Ogunquit, ME
Oklahoma City Museum of Art, Oklahoma City, OK
Peggy Guggenheim Collection, Venice, Italy
The Phillips Collection, Washington, DC
Rose Art Museum, Brandeis University, Waltham, MA
Seattle Art Museum, Seattle, WA
Smithsonian American Art Museum, Washington, DC
Solomon R. Guggenheim Museum, New York, NY
Staatliche Kunsthalle, Karlsruhe, Germany
Terra Museum of American Art, Chicago, IL
Wadsworth Atheneum Museum of Art, Hartford, CT
Whitney Museum of American Art, New York, NY
Worcester Art Museum, Worcester, MA

AWARDS

2003   Lee Krasner Lifetime Achievement Award given by the
      Pollock-Krasner Foundation

SOLO EXHIBITIONS

1945   *Charles Seliger: First Exhibition*, Art of This Century, New York, NY
1946   *Charles Seliger*, Art of This Century, New York, NY
1947   *Scarfs by Seliger: Hand Printed Silk*, Alexander Gerard Gallery,
      Gross Pointe, MI
1948   *Charles Seliger: Recent Paintings and Drawings*, Carlebach
      Gallery, New York, NY
      Paintings and Drawings of Charles Seliger, M.H. de Young
      Memorial Museum, San Francisco, CA
1949   *Drawings and Watercolors by Charles Seliger*, Research Studio,
      Maitland, FL
      The Magic of Line, Art Center School, Los Angeles, CA
      Carlebach Gallery, New York, NY
1951   *Charles Seliger*, Willard Gallery, New York, NY
1953   *Charles Seliger*, Willard Gallery, New York, NY
1954   *Charles Seliger*, Mount Vernon Art Center, Mt. Vernon, NY
1955   *Charles Seliger*, Willard Gallery, New York, NY; Otto Seligman
      Gallery, Seattle, WA
1957   *Charles Seliger: Oils, Temperas and Watercolors*, Willard Gallery,
      New York, NY
1958   *Paintings and Drawings by Charles Seliger*, Otto Seligman
      Gallery, Seattle, WA
1959   *Charles Seliger: Exhibition of Paintings*, Willard Gallery, New
      York, NY
1961   *Charles Seliger*, Willard Gallery, New York, NY
1962   *Charles Seliger: Exhibition of Recent Oil Paintings*, Willard Gallery,
      New York, NY
1963   *Charles Seliger*, Otto Seligman Gallery, Seattle, WA
1965   *Charles Seliger: Paintings and Drawings*, Otto Seligman Gallery,
      Seattle, WA
1966   *Charles Seliger*, Willard Gallery, New York, NY
      Charles Seliger, Nassau Community College, Garden City, NY
1967   *Charles Seliger*, Otto Seligman Gallery, Seattle, WA
1968   *Charles Seliger*, Willard Gallery, New York, NY
1969   *Seliger: Paintings and Drawings,* The Wooster School,
      Danbury, CT
1974   *Charles Seliger: Eidólons, 1973-74*, Andrew Crispo Gallery,
      New York, NY
1976   *Charles Seliger: Small Works on Canvas, 1970-76*, les Copains
      Art Ltd., Buffalo, NY
      Charles Seliger: Recent Paintings, Andrew Crispo Gallery,
      New York, NY
1978   *Charles Seliger: Aeons*, Andrew Crispo Gallery, New York, NY
      Charles Seliger: Recent Drawings, Andrew Crispo Gallery, New
      York, NY

1979 *Charles Seliger*, Makler Gallery, Philadelphia, PA
1980 *Seasons: A Selection of Small Paintings 1979-1980*, Andrew
Crispo Gallery, New York, NY
1981 *Charles Seliger: Intimate Abstractions*, Frances Wolfson Art
Gallery, Miami-Dade Community College, Miami, FL;
Jacksonville Art Museum, Jacksonville, FL
Charles Seliger: Origins, Andrew Crispo Gallery, New York, NY
1983 *Charles Seliger: Ways of Nature, Recent Paintings*, Andrew Crispo
Gallery, New York, NY
1985 *Charles Seliger: Eighteen Paintings*, Gallery Schlesinger-
Boisanté, New York, NY
1986 *Charles Seliger: Paintings and Works on Paper, 1949-1985*,
Solomon R. Guggenheim Museum, New York, NY
Charles Seliger, Galerie Lopes, Zurich, Switzerland
Charles Seliger: Recent Paintings, Watercolors, Monotypes,
Gallery Schlesinger-Boisanté, New York, NY
1987 *Charles Seliger: Recent Paintings, Watercolors, Monotypes*,
Gallery Schlesinger-Boisanté, New York, NY
1989 *Charles Seliger: Paintings and Works on Paper*, Galerie Lopes,
Zurich, Switzerland
1990 *Charles Seliger*, Saidenberg Gallery, New York, NY
Charles Seliger, Galerie Lopes, Zurich, Switzerland
1991 *Charles Seliger: Undercurrents, Watercolors*, Michael Rosenfeld
Gallery, New York, NY
1992 *Charles Seliger: Infinities, Recent Paintings*, Michael Rosenfeld
Gallery, New York, NY
1994 *Charles Seliger: Natures Journal - Recent Paintings and Gouaches*,
Michael Rosenfeld Gallery, New York, NY
1995 *Charles Seliger: The 1940s & 1990s*, Michael Rosenfeld
Gallery, New York, NY
1997 *Charles Seliger: Biomorphic Drawings, 1944-1947*, Michael
Rosenfeld Gallery, New York, NY
1999 *Charles Seliger: The Nascent Image, Recent Paintings*, Michael
Rosenfeld Gallery, New York, NY
2003 *Charles Seliger: Chaos to Complexity,* Michael Rosenfeld
Gallery, New York, NY
Charles Seliger: Sixty Years of Abstraction, Greenville County
Museum of Art, Greenville, SC
2006 *Charles Seliger: New Paintings,* Michael Rosenfeld Gallery,
New York, NY
2008 *Charles Seliger: Ways of Nature*, Michael Rosenfeld Gallery,
New York, NY

SELECTED GROUP EXHIBITIONS

1943 *Adventures in Perspective*, Norlyst Gallery, New York, NY
1944 *Captured Light: Experimental Paintings and Photography*,
Norlyst Gallery, New York, NY
Painters and Sculptors Society of New Jersey, Jersey City

Museum, Jersey City, NJ
40 American Moderns, 67 Gallery, New York, NY
1945 *Personal Statement: A Painting Prophecy*, The David Porter
Gallery, Washington, DC; Smith College Museum of Art,
Northampton, MA; City Art Museum, St. Louis, MO; San
Francisco Museum of Art, San Francisco, CA; The
Rochester Memorial Art Gallery, Rochester, NY
A Problem for Critics, 67 Gallery, New York, NY
Autumn Salon, Art of This Century, New York, NY
1946 *Abstract and Expressionist Painting*, Society of the Four Arts,
Palm Beach, FL
Fifth Biennial, Contemporary American Paintings, Virginia
Museum of Fine Arts, Richmond, VA
Five Young Americans, Art of This Century, New York, NY
Second Annual Contemporary Art, University of Iowa, Iowa
City, IO
1947 *Surrealist American Art*, Art Institute of Chicago, Chicago, IL
Third Annual Contemporary Art, University of Iowa, Iowa City,
IA
1948 *Realities Nouvelles*, Salon des Realites Nouvelles, Paris, France
New American Painters, Museum of Modern Art, New York, NY
Annual Contemporary American Paintings, Whitney Museum of
American Art, New York, NY; 1949, 51-58, 60
New Acquisitions, Museum of Modern Art, New York, NY
1949 *24th Venice Biennial*, Peggy Guggenheim Collection, Venice,
Italy
15th Biennial International Watercolor Exhibition, Brooklyn
Museum of Art, Brooklyn, NY; 1951, 57, 59
1950 *American Painting 1950*, Virginia Museum of Fine Arts,
Richmond, VA
American Painting and Sculpture, The Newark Museum,
Newark, NJ
Spiral Group, Riverside Museum, New York, NY
Barnyard Zoo, Baltimore Museum of Art, Baltimore, MD
1951 *Abstract Painting and Sculpture in America*, Museum of Modern
Art, New York, NY
Annual American Exhibition, Art Institute of Chicago, Chicago,
IL; 1955, 61, 62, 64
Young Painters USA, Cornell University, Ithaca, NY
Drawings, Willard Gallery, New York, NY
1952 *Contemporary Drawings from Twelve Countries*, Art Institute of
Chicago, Chicago, IL
Painter's Choice, Worcester Art Museum, Worcester, MA
Contemporary New Jersey Artists, The Newark Museum,
Newark, NJ
Land, Sea and Air, The Children's Museum, Denver, CO
1953 *Abstract Painting in America*, Syracuse Museum of Fine Arts,
Syracuse, NY

63rd Annual Exhibition, Nebraska Art Association, Lincoln, NB

1954 *American Painting 1954*, Virginia Museum of Fine Arts, Richmond, VA

American Painting 1954, Des Moines Art Center, Des Moines, IA

1955 *Contemporary American and European Paintings*, Columbus Museum of Fine Arts, Columbus, OH

Pittsburgh International, Carnegie Institute, Pittsburgh, PA

Contemporary American and European Paintings, John Herron Art Museum, Indianapolis, IN

1956 *Recent Accessions*, Wadsworth Atheneum, Hartford, CT

1957 *New York Artists 6th Annual Exhibition*, Stable Gallery, New York, NY

L'Arte Grafica Contemporanea, Stati Uniti, Gallerie Nazionale d'Arte Moderna, Rome, Italy

Twentieth Century American Graphic Arts, United States Information Agency (traveled)

Edward Wales Root, An American Collector, Munson-Williams-Proctor Institute, Utica, NY; Addison Gallery of American Art, Andover, MA; University of Michigan Museum of Art, Ann Arbor, MI

1958 *75th Annual Exhibition*, Portland Museum of Art, Portland, ME

The New Landscape in Art and Science, The American Federation of the Arts, New York, NY

3rd Annual Exhibition of Contemporary Painting, Dupont Galleries, Mary Washington College of the University of Virginia, Fredericksburg, VA

1959 *Contemporary American Watercolors*, John Herron Art Museum, Indianapolis, IN

National Drawing Competition, Boston Museum of Fine Arts, Boston, MA

4th Exhibition of Modern Art, Mary Washington College of the University of Virginia, Fredericksburg, VA

Selected Drawings from National Drawing Competition, DeCordova Museum and Sculpture Park, Lincoln, MA

1960 *The Importance of the Small Painting*, The Nordness Gallery, New York, NY

1961 *The Quest and the Quarry*, Rome-New York Art Foundation, Rome, Italy

Ninth Annual Exhibition, Ogunquit Museum of Art, Ogunquit, ME

Sixth Exhibition of Modern Art, Mary Washington College of the University of Virginia, Fredericksburg, VA

1962 *157th Annual Exhibition of American Painting and Sculpture*, Pennsylvania Academy of the Fine Arts, Philadelphia, PA

Edward R. Root Bequest, Munson-Williams-Proctor Institute, Utica, NY

Three Painters, Haydon Calhoun Galleries, Dallas, TX

New Accessions USA, Colorado Springs Fine Arts Center, Colorado Springs, CO

1963 *Art for American Embassies*, Department of State, Washington, DC

Contemporary Masters Drawings and Prints, Providence Art Club, Providence, RI

1964 *Watercolors and Drawings*, Munson-Williams-Proctor Institute, Utica, NY

1965 *Contemporary American Paintings and Sculpture*, University of Illinois, Urbana, IL

10th Exhibition of Modern Art, Mary Washington College of the University of Virginia, Fredericksburg, VA

1966 *Selections from the Permanent Collection*, Rose Art Museum, Brandeis University, Waltham, MA

Drawings USA '66, 3rd Biennial Exhibition, Saint Paul Art Center, St. Paul, MN

Childe Hassam and Eugene Speicher Purchase Fund Exhibition, American Academy of Arts and Letters, New York, NY

1967 *XXII American Drawing Biennial*, Norfolk Museum of Fine Arts and Sciences, Norfolk, VA

1968 *The Art of the Organic Forms*, National Collection of Fine Arts, Smithsonian Institution, Washington, DC

Childe Hassam and Eugene Speicher Purchase Fund Exhibition, American Academy of Arts and Letters, New York, NY

1970 *Miniaturan '70 International*, Galerie 66 HG, Hofheim, West Germany

Art for Peace, Laguardia Place, New York, NY

1975 *20th Century American Painting and Sculpture*, Andrew Crispo Gallery, New York, NY

1976 *20th Century American Masters*, Andrew Crispo Gallery, New York, NY

Watercolors: Historical and Contemporary, Skidmore College, Saratoga Springs, NY

1977 *This Is Today: An Exhibition of Works by Living Artists*, Root Center, Hamilton College, Clinton, NY

Members' Gallery, Albright-Knox Art Gallery, Buffalo, NY

Recent Acquisitions, Solomon R. Guggenheim Museum, New York, NY

1979 *Works on Paper, USA*, Rockland Center for the Arts, West Nyack, NY

1981 *New York Gallery Showcase*, Oklahoma Art Center, Oklahoma, OK

Contemporary American Landscape, Taft Museum, Cincinnati, OH

Bouquet, Summit Art Center, Summit, NJ

1982 *Solitude, Inner Visions in American Art*, Terra Museum of American Art, Chicago, IL

Drawings by Picasso and Paul Klee, Abstractions by Charles Seliger,

Saidenberg Gallery, New York, NY
The Spirit of Paper: 20th Century American, Frances Wolfson Art Gallery, Miami, FL
Lowell Nesbitt, Charles Seliger, Douglas Abdell, Tirca Karlis Gallery, Provincetown, MA

1986 *50th Anniversary Exhibition in Memory of Marian Willard Johnson*, Willard Gallery, New York, NY

1987 *Peggy Guggenheim's Other Legacy*, Solomon R. Guggenheim Museum, New York; The Peggy Guggenheim Collection, Venice, Italy
Nature Into Art, Artists in Depth, Munson-Williams-Proctor Institute, Utica, NY
Watercolor Now! Paintings by Linda Chapman, Richard Frank, Juan Pastorelli, Charles Seliger, Frances Wolfson Art Gallery, Miami-Dade Community College, Miami, FL
Visions of Inner Space: Gestural Painting in Modern American Art, Wright Art Gallery, University of California, Los Angeles, CA; National Gallery of Modern Art, New Delhi, India
Inaugural Exhibition, Sid Deutsch Gallery, New York, NY

1989 *Abstract Expressionism, Other Dimensions*, Lowe Art Museum, University of Miami, Coral Gables, FL; Terra Museum of American Art, Chicago, IL; Jane Voorhees Zimmerli Art Museum, Rutgers University, New Brunswick, NJ; Whitney Museum of American Art, Philip Morris Branch, New York, NY
Late 19th and 20th Century American Masters, Sid Deutsch Gallery, New York, NY
Art on Paper 1989, Weatherspoon Art Gallery, University of North Carolina, Greensboro, NC
Works on Paper, Sid Deutsch Gallery, New York, NY
Gyorgy Kepes, Herbert Bayer, Charles Seliger: Paintings and Works on Paper, Saidenberg Gallery, New York, NY

1990 *Watercolors from the Abstract Expressionist Era*, Katonah Art Museum, Katonah, NY
An Artist's Christmas, Holiday Images of American Artists 1880-1990, Midtown Payson Galleries, New York, NY

1991 *Watercolor Across the Ages*, Bristol-Myers Squibb Gallery, Princeton, NJ
Nature's Rhythm, Snyder Fine Art, New York, NY
Stamens and Pistils: Interpreting the Flower 1790-1990, Louis Stern Galleries, Beverly Hills, CA

1992 *Theme & Improvisation: Kandinsky and the American Avant-Garde, 1912-1950*, Terra Museum of American Art, Chicago, IL; The Phillips Collection, Washington, DC; Amon Carter Museum, Fort Worth, TX; Dayton Art Institute, Dayton, OH

1993 *Expression Abstracted: 35 Memory Portraits*, Zimmerli Art Museum, Rutgers University, New Brunswick, NJ

Lines & Myths: Abstraction in American Art, 1941-51, Michael Rosenfeld Gallery, New York, NY
Aspects of American Abstraction, 1930-42, Michael Rosenfeld Gallery, New York, NY

1994 *On Paper: Abstraction in America*, Michael Rosenfeld Gallery, New York, NY

1995 *Collage: Made in America*, Michael Rosenfeld Gallery, New York, NY
Exploring the Unknown: Surrealism in American Art, Michael Rosenfeld Gallery, New York, NY
A Twentieth Century Survey of American Watercolor, Southern Alleghenies Museum of Art, Loretto, PA
Surrealism in Exile, La Maison Francaise, New York University, New York, NY

1997 *Surrealism and American Art 1932-1949*, The Boca Raton Museum of Art, Boca Raton, FL

1998 *The Surrealist Vision: Europe and the Americas*, Bruce Museum, Greenwich, CT
Original Scale, Apex Art C.P., New York, NY
Essence of the Orb, Michael Rosenfeld Gallery, New York, NY
Peggy Guggenheim: A Centennial Celebration, Solomon R. Guggenheim Museum, New York, NY
Surrealism in America During the 1930s and 1940s: Selections from the Penny and Elton Yasuna Collection, Salvador Dali Museum, St. Petersburg, FL
The Surrealists in Exile and the Origin of the New York School, Museo Nacional Centro de Arte Reina Sofía, Madrid, Spain; Musées d'Art Moderne et Contemporain, Strasbourg, Germany
Severed Ear: The Poetry of Abstraction, The Creiger-Dane Gallery, Boston, MA
Paper Invitational II, Woodward Gallery, New York, NY
Linear Impulse, Michael Rosenfeld Gallery, New York, NY
Calm and Commotion: Abstract Art from the Permanent Collection, Mississippi Museum of Art, Jackson, MS
Impossible Landscapes of the Mind, Hirschl & Adler Galleries, New York, NY

2000 *Bug Out*, Munson-Williams-Proctor Arts Institute, Utica, NY
Michael Rosenfeld Gallery: The First Decade, Michael Rosenfeld Gallery, New York, NY

2001 *Jazz and Visual Improvisation*, Katonah Art Museum, Katonah, NY
Flora: In Reverence of Nature, Michael Rosenfeld Gallery, New York, NY
Paper Assets: Collecting Prints and Drawings, 1996-2000, The British Museum, London, England
Vital Forms: American Art and Design in the Atomic Age, 1940-1960, Brooklyn Museum of Art, Brooklyn, NY; Walker Art

Center, Minneapolis, MN; Frist Center for the Visual Arts, Nashville, TN; Phoenix Art Museum, Phoenix, AZ

1950-65: Abstraction on Paper, Michael Rosenfeld Gallery, New York, NY

2002   *Transitions at Mid-Century, Works on Paper 1945-1955*, Whitney Museum of American Art, New York, NY

2003   *On Paper: Masterworks from the Addison Collection*, Addison Gallery of American Art, Andover, MA

The Art of Organic Forms, Michael Rosenfeld Gallery, New York, NY

Graphic Masters: Highlights from the Smithsonian American Art Museum, Heckscher Museum of Art, Huntington, NY; Palmer Museum of Art, Pennsylvania State University, University Park, PA; Hunter Museum of American Art, Chattanooga, TN; Plains Art Museum, Fargo, ND

Peggy and Kiesler: The Collection and the Visionary, Peggy Guggenheim Collection, Venice, Italy

The 1940s: Modern American Art & Design, Michael Rosenfeld Gallery, New York, NY

In Sequence, Michael Rosenfeld Gallery, New York, NY

Surrealism & Modernism from the Collection of the Wadsworth Atheneum Museum of Art, The Phillips Collection, Washington, DC; Orange County Museum of Art, Newport Beach, CA; Kimbell Art Museum, Fort Worth, TX; The John and Mable Ringling Museum of Art, Sarasota, FL

2004   *Endless Love*, DC Moore Gallery, New York, NY

2005   *Surrealism USA*, National Academy Museum, New York, NY; Phoenix Art Museum, Phoenix, AZ

Organic New York, 1941-1949, Michael Rosenfeld Gallery, New York, NY

Dalí, Picasso and the Surrealist Vision, Wadsworth Atheneum Museum of Art, Hartford, CT

2006   *American Modernism on Paper*, Michael Rosenfeld Gallery, New York, NY

Pre–Post, Greenberg Van Doren Gallery, New York, NY

2007   *Pathways and Parallels: Roads to Abstract Expressionism*, Hollis Taggart Galleries, New York, NY

Shining Spirit: Westheimer Family Collection, Oklahoma City Museum of Art, Oklahoma City, OK

Auspicious Vision: Edward Wales Root & American Art, Munson-Williams-Proctor Institute, Utica, NY

Surrealism: Dreams on Canvas, Nassau County Museum of Art, Roslyn Harbor, NY

2008   *Abstract Expressionism: A World Elsewhere,* Haunch of Venison, New York, NY

MICHAEL ROSENFELD GALLERY
PUBLICATIONS

Abstraction Across America, 1934-1946, AAA and Transcendentalists...........................essays by Ed Garman and Hananiah Harari

African American Art: 200 Years ....essays by Jonathan P. Binstock and Dr. Lowery Stokes Sims

African-American Art: 20th Century Masterworks...essay by Beryl Wright

African-American Art: 20th Century Masterworks, II ....foreword by Harold B. Nelson, essay by Professor Richard J. Powell

African-American Art: 20th Century Masterworks, III ....essay by Michael Rosenfeld

African-American Art: 20th Century Masterworks, IV ....forewords by Kevin Grogan and Michael Rosenfeld

African-American Art: 20th Century Masterworks, V ....foreword by Nancy Corwin, essay by Dr. Leslie King-Hammond

African-American Art: 20th Century Masterworks, VI ....essay by Michael Rosenfeld

African-American Art: 20th Century Masterworks, VII ....foreword by Jeffrey Spalding, essay by halley k harrisburg

African-American Art: 20th Century Masterworks, VIII ....foreword by Dr. Alvia J. Wardlaw statements by several artists

African-American Art: 20th Century Masterworks, IX.......................................foreword by Carey Pickard, essay by Dr. Leslie King-Hammond

African-American Art: 20th Century Masterworks, X..essay by Professor Robin D. G. Kelley

Aspects of American Abstraction: 1930-1942 ....essay by Dr. Gail Stavitsky

Romare Bearden – Fractured Tales: Intimate Collages.....................................essay by Romare Bearden (1968 reprint)

Benjamin Benno: 1930s American Modernist in Paris ....essay by Donna Gustafson

John Biggers: My America ....foreword by Whitfield Lovell, introduction by Michael Rosenfeld

Body Beware: 18 American Artists ....statement by Professor Jessica Scarlata

Byron Browne: Evolution of an American Modernist, 1930s-50s ....essay by Professor Matthew Baigell

Federico Castellon: Surrealist Paintings Rediscovered, 1933-1934..................essay by Paul Cummings

Federico Castellon: Surrealist Drawings of the 1930s ....statement by Michael Rosenfeld

Counterpoints: American Art, 1930-1945 ....essay by Michael Rosenfeld

Jay DeFeo: Her Tripod and Its Dress..essay by Elisabeth Sussman

Jay DeFeo: Ingredients of Alchemy, Before and After The Rose ....foreword by Lisa Phillips, essay by Carter Ratcliff

Defining the Edge: Early American Abstraction, Selections from the
Collection of Dr. Peter B. Fischer ....essay by Dr. Gail Stavitsky with selected artist quotes

Beauford Delaney: Liquid Light – Paris Abstractions, 1954-1970....................essay by Professor David Leeming

Burgoyne Diller: Collages ....essay by Dr. Susan C. Larsen

Burgoyne Diller: The Third Dimension, Sculpture & Drawings, 1930-1965.......essay by Michael Rosenfeld

Burgoyne Diller: The 1960s ....essay by Barry Schwabsky

Burgoyne Diller: The 1930s, Cubism to Abstraction ....essay by Dr. Francis V. O'Connor

Embracing the Muse: Africa and African American Art ....essay by Dr. Nnamdi Elleh

Exploring the Unknown: Surrealism in American Art.......................................essay by Michael Rosenfeld

Essence of the Orb ....statement by Michael Rosenfeld with selected artist quotes

Eye Contact ....pictorial essay

Fiber and Form: The Woman's Legacy ....foreword by halley k harrisburg

Morris Graves: Toward an Ultimate Reality ....selected artist quotes

Nancy Grossman: Loud Whispers, Four Decades of Assemblage,
Collage and Sculpture ....foreword by Thomas W. Styron, essay by Dr. Lowery Stokes Sims

Blanche Lazzell: American Modernist ....essay by Michael Rosenfeld and halley k harrisburg

Norman Lewis: Intuitive Markings ....selected artist quotes

Linear Impulse ....statement by Michael Rosenfeld with selected artist quotes

Lines & Myths: Abstraction in American Art, 1941-1951 ....essay by Professor Melvin P. Lader

Seymour Lipton: Abstract Expressionist Sculptor..essay by Martica Sawin

Martha Madigan: Seeds of Light from the Human Nature Series......................essay by Charles Hagen

Martha Madigan: Vernal Equinox, Recent Photograms ....essay by A. D. Coleman

Boris Margo: Surrealism to Abstraction, 1932-1952 ....essay by Jeffrey Wechsler

Michael Rosenfeld Gallery: The First Decade...essay by Michael Rosenfeld and halley k harrisburg

Clifford Odets: In Hell + Why, Paintings on Paper ....essay by Michael Rosenfeld and Harold Clurman Odets' eulogy

Clifford Odets, It's Your Birthday!...chronology by halley k harrisburg

Clifford Odets: Paradise Lost, Paintings on Paper ....essay by J. Hoberman

Organic New York, 1941-1949 ....essay by Robert C. Morgan

Alfonso Ossorio: Horror Vacui..foreword by Mike Solomon, essay by Helen Harrison

Alfonso Ossorio: Masterworks from the Collection of the

Robert U. Ossorio Foundation ....foreword by Frederic E. Ossorio, Jr., introduction by Harry Cooper

Alfonso Ossorio: Reflection & Redemption — The Surrealist Decade ....essay by Professor Ellen Landau

Alfonso Ossorio: Road ....essay by B.H. Friedmaan

Alfonso Ossorio: The Child Returns: 1950-Philippines, Expressionist Paintings on Paper .essay by Dr. Francis V. O'Connor

Alfonso Ossorio: The Creeks: Before, During and After...essay by Mike Solomon

Alfonso Ossorio: The Shingle Figures ....essay by B.H. Friedman

Out of the Fifties – Into the Sixties, 6 Figurative Expressionists ....essay by Michael Rosenfeld

Perceivable Realities: Eilshemius, Graves, Tanner, Tchelitchew ....statement by Michael Rosenfeld

Betye Saar: Colored, Consider the Rainbow ....essay by Dr. Leslie King-Hammond

Betye Saar: In Service, A Version of Survival...essay by Dr. Lizzetta LeFalle-Collins

Betye Saar: Migrations/Transformations...essays by Whitfield Lovell, Tracye Saar-Cavanaugh,

                                                                                                        Lowery Stokes Sims, Sean M. Ulmer

Betye Saar: Workers + Warriors, The Return of Aunt Jemima ....essay by Dr. Arlene Raven

Charles Seliger: Biomorphic Drawings, 1944-1947 ....essay by Sam Hunter

Charles Seliger: Chaos to Complexity..essay by John Yau

Charles Seliger: Infinities ....essay by Addison Parks

Charles Seliger: Nature's Journal ....essay by Professor Gail Levin

Charles Seliger: Ways of Nature...essay by Michelle DuBois

Charles Seliger: The Nascent Image—Recent Paintings ....foreword by Roald Hoffmann and an interview with the artist

                                                                                                        by halley k harrisburg

Charles Seliger: New Paintings ....foreword by James Siena, essay by Isabelle Dervaux

Charles G. Shaw..introduction by Michael Rosenfeld, essay by Debra Bricker Balken

Theodoros Stamos: Allegories of Nature, 1946-1949 ....essay by Barbara Cavaliere

Louis Stone: American Modernist ....essay by Joseph Jacobs

Louis Stone: The Path to Abstraction (1928-1945)..essay by Joseph Jacobs

Stroke! Beauford Delaney, Norman Lewis and Alma Thomas ....essay by Dr. Lowery Stokes Sims

Surrealism Embodied: The Figure in American Art, 1933-1953 ....essay by Jeffrey Wechsler

Lenore Tawney: Meditations – Assemblages, Collages & Weavings ....essay by Dr. Judith Stein

Pavel Tchelitchew: Nature Transformed..interview with Charles Henri Ford by Paul Cummings

Pavel Tchelitchew: Nature Within & Without..essay by Paul Cummings

Alma Thomas: Phantasmagoria, Major Paintings of the 1970s......................................foreword by Victoria Montelongo,

                                                                                                        essay by Dr. Lowery Stokes Sims

Bob Thompson: Fantastic Visions, Paintings & Drawings..statement by Carol Thompson

Bob Thompson: Heroes, Martyrs & Spectres...statement by Michael Rosenfeld

Bob Thompson: Meteor in a Black Hat...introduction and essay by Stanley Crouch

The Transcendental Painting Group: Major Paintings ....essay by halley k harrisburg

True Grit...essay by Dr. Arlene Raven

Charmion von Wiegand: Offering of the Universe:

An Artist's Path from Mondrian to Mantra ....foreword by Helen Tworkov, essay by

                                                                                                        Stephen Westfall

Charmion von Wiegand: Spirit & Form—Collages, 1946-1961.......................................essay by Dr. Susan C. Larsen

Charmion von Wiegand: Spirituality in Abstraction, 1945-1969 ....essay by Dr. Jennifer Newton Hersh

Charmion von Wiegand: 1945—Improvisations ....essay by Professor William C. Agee

The WPA Era: Urban Views & Visions ....essay by Dr. Francis V. O'Connor

James VanDerZee: Harlem Guaranteed ....essays by Hilton Als and Dr. Cheryl Finley

To purchase catalogues, please visit www.michaelrosenfeldart.com

MICHAEL ROSENFELD GALLERY
EXHIBITION HISTORY

A Selection of Twentieth Century American Art . . . . .December 10, 1989–March 25, 1990

Surrealism & Magic Realism in American Art . . . . .April 1–June 1, 1990

Raphael & Moses Soyer . . . . .June 4–July 20, 1990

Dwinell Grant: Drawings for "Contrathemis" . . . . .September 4–October 6, 1990

Figures of Speech: Social Realism of the WPA Era . . . . .October 9–November 17, 1990

Charles Seliger: Undercurrents . . . . .February 5–March 9, 1991

American Abstract Artists: 1930s & 1940s . . . . .March 14–April 27, 1991

Benjamin Benno: 1930s American Modernist in Paris . . . . .May 4–June 15, 1991

Byron Browne: Evolution of an American Modernist, 1930s-1950s . . . . .September 21–October 26, 1991

Pavel Tchelitchew: Nature Within & Without . . . . .October 31–December 14, 1991

Surrealism Embodied: The Figure in American Art, 1933-1953 . . . . .February 13–March 28, 1992

Charles Seliger: Infinities, Recent Paintings . . . . .April 4–May 9, 1992

The WPA Era: Urban Views & Visions . . . . .May 12–June 27, 1992

Federico Castellon: Surrealist Paintings Rediscovered, 1933-1934 . . . . .September 12–October 31, 1992

Lines & Myths: Abstraction in American Art, 1941-1951 . . . . .November 5–January 20, 1993

Aspects of American Abstraction, 1930-1942 . . . . .February 11–March 27, 1993

Pavel Tchelitchew: Nature Transformed . . . . .April 3–May 29, 1993

On Paper: The Figure in 20th Century American Art . . . . .June 10–August 15, 1993

Boris Margo: Surrealism to Abstraction, 1930-1952 traveled to Center for the Arts, Vero Beach, FL . . . . .September 31–November 12, 1993

African-American Art: 20th Century Masterworks . . . . .November 18–February 12, 1994

Charles Seliger: Nature's Journals, Recent Paintings and Gouaches . . . . .February 19–April 2, 1994

Counterpoints: American Art, 1930-1945 . . . . .April 7–June 4, 1994

On Paper: Abstraction in American Art . . . . .June 9–August 12, 1994

Perceivable Realities: Eilshemius, Graves, Tanner and Tchelitchew . . . . .September 22–November 10, 1994

Gallery II: Martha Madigan: Human Nature . . . . .September 22–November 10, 1994

Planes, Trains & Automobiles: Machine-Age America . . . . .November 17–January 22, 1995

Gallery II: Irene Rice Pereira: Monumental Paintings, 1932-1938 . . . . .November 17–January 22, 1995

African-American Art: 20th Century Masterworks, II traveled to Long Beach Museum of Art, Long Beach, CA . . February 1–April 8, 1995

Burgoyne Diller: A Pioneer of Abstraction . . . . .April 13–June 3, 1995

Gallery II: Charles Seliger: The 1940s & 1990s . . . . .April 13–June 3, 1995

Collage: Made in America . . . . .June 8–August 25, 1995

Gallery II: Fairfield Porter: Drawings and Poetry . . . . .June 8–August 25, 1995

William H. Johnson: Works from the Collection of Mary Beattie Brady . . . . .September 14–November 11, 1995

Gallery II: Beauford Delaney: Paris Abstractions from the 1960s . . . . .September 14–November 11, 1995

Exploring the Unknown: Surrealism in American Art . . . . .November 16–January 27, 1996

Gallery II: Boris Margo: Fantasy in Form . . . . .November 16–January 27, 1996

African-American Art: 20th Century Masterworks, III . . . . .January 31–April 6, 1996

Clifford Odets: In Hell + Why: Paintings 1940s & 1950s traveled to Oregon
Shakespeare Festival, Ashland, OR; Williams College Museum of Art,
Williamstown, MA . . . . .April 11–June 8, 1996

Gallery II: We The People! American Voices of the WPA Era . . . . .April 11–June 8, 1996

Fiber and Form: The Woman's Legacy . . . . .June 13–September 3, 1996

Abstraction Across America: American Abstract Artists & Transcendentalists . . . . .September 11–November 9, 1996

Reflection & Redemption: The Surrealist Decade of Alfonso Ossorio, 1939-49 traveled to
Greenville County Museum of Art, Greenville, SC . . . . .November 14–January 18, 1997

Gallery II: Federico Castellon: Surrealist Drawings of the 1930s . . . . .November 14–January 18, 1997

African-American Art: 20th Century Masterworks, IV traveled to
Fisk University Galleries, Nashville, TN . . . . .January 23–March 26, 1997

Lenore Tawney: Meditations—Assemblages, Collages & Weavings . . . . .April 2–May 31, 1997

Gallery II: Martha Madigan: Seeds of Light from the Human Nature Series . . . . .April 2–May 31, 1997

Facets of the Figure: A Spectrum of 20th Century American Art . . . . .June 5–August 22, 1997

Gallery II: Charles Seliger: Biomorphic Drawings, 1944-1947 . . . . .June 5–August 22, 1997

Bob Thompson: Heroes, Martyrs & Spectres . . . . .September 11–November 8, 1997

Gallery II: Alfonso Ossorio: The Shingle Figures, 1962-1963 . . . . .September 11–November 8, 1997

Burgoyne Diller: The Third Dimension, Sculpture & Drawings, 1930-1965 . . . . .November 13–January 17, 1998

Gallery II: The New Frontier: Early American Moderns . . . . .November 13–January 17, 1998

African-American Art: 20th Century Masterworks, V traveled to

The Newcomb Art Gallery, Tulane University, New Orleans, LA . . . . .January 22–March 21, 1998

Defining the Edge: Early American Abstraction, Selections from the Collection of Dr. Peter B. Fischer

traveled to The Laguna Art Museum,

Laguna, CA . . . . .March 26–May 30, 1998

Essence of the Orb . . . . .June 4–August 20, 1998

Gallery II: Boris Margo: Divine Light, 1950-1952 . . . . .June 4–August 20, 1998

Alfonso Ossorio: Master Prints, 1932-1990 at Ossorio Foundation, Southampton, NY . . . . .June 20–September 6, 1998

Betye Saar: Workers + Warriors: The Return of Aunt Jemima traveled

to Greenville County Museum of Art, Greenville, SC; Detroit Institute of Arts, Detroit, MI . . . . .September 10–October 31, 1998

Gallery II: Spirit & Form: Charmion von Wiegand: Collages, 1946-1961 . . . . .September 10–October 31, 1998

Alfonso Ossorio, The Child Returns: 1950-Philippines, Expressionist Paintings on Paper . . . . .November 5, 1998–January 9, 1999

Gallery II: Bob Thompson: Fantastic Visions, Paintings & Drawings . . . . .November 5, 1998–January 9, 1999

African-American Art: 20th Century Masterworks, VI traveled to

Flint Institute of Arts, Flint, MI . . . . .January 14–March 6, 1999

Charles Seliger: The Nascent Image, Recent Paintings . . . . .March 11–May 1, 1999

Gallery II: Morris Graves: Toward an Ultimate Reality . . . . .March 11–May 1, 1999

Linear Impulse May 6–August 13, 1999

Gallery II: Norman Lewis—Intuitive Markings, Works on Paper, 1945-1975 . . . . .May 6–August 13, 1999

Alfonso Ossorio: Costume Designs from the 1930s & 1940s for Ballet and Greek Tragedies at

Ossorio Foundation, Southampton, NY traveled to Mississippi Museum of At, Jackson, MS . . . . .June 5–September 7, 1999

Beauford Delaney: Liquid Light—Paris Abstractions, 1954-1970 . . . . .September 10–October 30, 1999

Harold Cousins: The 1950s—Welded Sculpture . . . . .September 10–October 30, 1999

Burgoyne Diller: Collages . . . . .November 4, 1999–January 8, 2000

Gallery II: The Transcendental Painting Group . . . . .November 4, 1999–January 8, 2000

African-American Art: 20th Century Masterworks, VII traveled to Appleton Museum of Art, Ocala, FL . . . . .January 13–March 4, 2000

True Grit traveled to Mills College Art Gallery, Oakland, CA; Boise Museum of Art, Boise, ID;

Marsh Art Gallery, University of Richmond, Richmond, VA; Farnsworth Art Museum, Rockland, ME;

El Paso Museum of Art, El Paso, TX; Newcomb Art Gallery, Tulane University, New Orleans, LA;

Center for the Visual Arts, Metropolitan State College, Denver, CO . . . . .March 9–May 6, 2000

Gallery II: Betye Saar: In Service, A Version of Survival . . . . .March 9–May 6, 2000

Michael Rosenfeld Gallery: The First Decade . . . . .May 11–August 10, 2000

Alfonso Ossorio: The Creeks—Before, During and After at Ossorio

Foundation, Southampton, NY . . . . .June 1–September 4, 2000

Charmion von Wiegand: Spirituality in Abstraction, 1945-1969 . . . . .September 7–October 28, 2000

Gallery II: Blanche Lazzell: American Modernist . . . . .September 7–October 28, 2000

Nancy Grossman: Loud Whispers traveled to The Greenville County Museum of Art, Greenville, SC;

Savannah College of Art and Design, Savannah, GA . . . . .November 2, 2000–January 13, 2001

Gallery II: Sensual Lines: American Figurative Drawings . . . . .November 2, 2000–January 13, 2001

African-American Art: 20th Century Masterworks, VIII

traveled to Texas Southern University Museum, Houston, TX . . . . .January 18–March 10, 2001

Out of the Fifties—Into the Sixties: 6 Figurative Expressionists . . . . .March 15–May 5, 2001

Martha Madigan: Vernal Equinox, Recent Photograms . . . . .May 9–June 30, 2001

Gallery II: Flora: In Reverence of Nature . . . . .May 9–June 30, 2001

Synergy: Alfonso Ossorio and Jackson Pollock, 1950-1951 at Ossorio Foundation, Southampton, NY

traveled to Federal Reserve Fine Arts Program, Washington, DC . . . . June 1–September 2, 2001

Alma Thomas: Phantasmagoria, Major Paintings traveled to The Women's Museum, Dallas, TX . . . . September 13–November 3, 2001

Gallery II: Abstraction on Paper, 1950–1965 . . . . September 13–November 3, 2001

Burgoyne Diller: The 1930s, Cubism to Abstraction . . . . Nov. 8, 2001–January 12, 2002

Gallery II: Theodoros Stamos: Allegories of Nature, Organic Abstractions

traveled to Asheville Art Museum, Asheville, NC . . . . Nov. 8, 2001–January 12, 2002

African-American Art: 20th Century Masterworks, IX traveled to Tubman

AfricanAmerican Museum, Macon, GA . . . . January 17–March 9, 2002

Jay DeFeo: Ingredients of Alchemy, Before and After The Rose . . . . March 14–May 4, 2002

Alfonso Ossorio: Horror Vacui . . . . May 9–July 29, 2002

Alfonso Ossorio: Horror Vacui at Ossorio Foundation, Southampton, NY . . . . May 30–September 1, 2002

Gallery II: Clifford Odets: Paradise Lost, Paintings on Paper . . . . May 9–July 29, 2002

Betye Saar: Colored—Consider the Rainbow traveled to The Columbus

Museum Uptown, Columbus, GA . . . . September 12–November 2, 2002

Louis Stone: American Modernist, Major Paintings 1930-1942 . . . . Nov. 7, 2002–January 11, 2003

Gallery II: Early American Abstraction: Small Scale—Large Dimension . . . . Nov. 7, 2002–January 11, 2003

African-American Art: 20th Century Masterworks, X . . . . January 16–March 8, 2003

Charles Seliger: Chaos to Complexity . . . . March 13–May 3, 2003

Gallery II: The Art of Organic Forms . . . . March 13–May 3, 2003

American Identity: Figurative Painting and Sculpture, 1930–1945 . . . . May 9–July 11, 2003

Gallery II: Ben Shahn: Freedom of Speech . . . . May 9–July 11, 2003

Charmion von Wiegand: Improvisations - 1945 . . . . September 9–November 1, 2003

Gallery II: The 1940s: Modern American Art & Design . . . . September 9–November 1, 2003

Jay DeFeo: Her Tripod and Its Dress . . . . Nov. 6, 2003–January 10, 2004

Gallery II: In Sequence: Lee Bontecou, Jay DeFeo, Burgoyne Diller,

Alfred Jensen, Anne Ryan, Charles Seliger and Charmion von Wiegand . . . . Nov. 6, 2003–January 10, 2004

Embracing the Muse: Africa and African American Art . . . . January 15–March 13, 2004

Burgoyne Diller: The 1960s . . . . March 18–May 15, 2004

Mood Indigo: The Legacy of Duke Ellington (A Look at Jazz and

Improvisation in American Art) . . . . May 20–July 30, 2004

Breaking Boundaries: American Abstract Art (1930-1945) . . . . Sept. 10, 2004–October 30, 2004

Gallery II: The 1930s: Modern American Art & Design . . . . Sept. 10, 2004–October 30, 2004

John Biggers: My America, The 1940s and 1950s traveled to the

New Orleans Museum of Art, New Orleans, LA . . . . Nov. 5, 2004–January 8, 2005

Stroke! Beauford Delaney, Norman Lewis & Alma Thomas . . . . January 14–March 12, 2005

Seymour Lipton: Abstract Expressionist Sculptor . . . . March 18–May 14, 2005

Eye Contact . . . . May 20–August 5, 2005

Organic New York, 1941-1949 . . . . September 10–November 5, 2005

Gallery II: Burgoyne Diller: Twenty-Five on Paper . . . . September 10–November 5, 2005

Bob Thompson: Meteor in a Black Hat, traveled to Haggerty Museum of Art,

Marquette University, Milwaukee, WI . . . . Nov. 11, 2005–January 7, 2006

Building Community: The African American Scene . . . . January 13–March 11, 2006

Charles Seliger: New Paintings . . . . March 17–May 13, 2006

Gallery II: American Modernism on Paper . . . . March 17–May 13, 2006

It's Your Birthday, Clifford Odets! A Centennial Exhibition . . . . May 19–August 4, 2006

Gallery II: Heartland: The American Scene . . . . May 19–August 4, 2006

Betye Saar: Migrations/Transformations . . . . September 8–October 28, 2006

Gallery II: Romare Bearden – Fractured Tales: Intimate Collages . . . . September 8–October 28, 2006

Louis Stone: The Path to Abstraction, 1928-1945 ....November 3–December 22, 2006
Decoding Myth: African American Abstraction, 1945-1975 ....January 6–March 10, 2007
Charmion von Wiegand: Offering of the Universe:
An Artist's Path from Mondrian to Mantra ....March 15–May 12, 2007
Body Beware: 16 American Artists ....May 18–July 27, 2007
Gallery II: Nancy Grossman: Drawings...May 18–July 27, 2007
Alfonso Ossorio: Masterworks from the Collection of
The Robert U. Ossorio Foundation ....September 8–October 27, 2007
Charles G. Shaw ....November 1–December 22, 2007
African American Art: 200 Years ....January 10–March 15, 2008
Seymour Lipton: Metal ....March 20–May 17, 2008
(un)common threads ....May 23–July 31, 2008
Charles Seliger: Ways of Nature ....September 6–October 25, 2008
Gallery II: Theodore Roszak ....September 6–October 25, 2008
Irving Norman ....October 30–December 20, 2008

CREDITS

Exhibition Coordinator
halley k harrisburg
Bruce Kriegel

Catalogue Design and Editor
halley k harrisburg

Catalogue Essay
© Michelle DuBois

Essay Editor
Jessica Scarlata

Catalogue Photography
Joshua Nefsky

Catalogue Art Direction and Production
CP Design

Catalogue Typeface
Magma

Catalogue Printing
Oceanic Graphic Printing, Inc.

Printed in China
Edition 1500
ISBN #1-930416-44-X

© Michael Rosenfeld Gallery
24 West 57 Street, 7ᵗʰ Floor
New York, NY 10019
(212) 247-0082 / (212) 247-0402 fax
www.michaelrosenfeldart.com

Gallery Hours:
Tuesday through Saturday, 10:00-6:00 pm

On the cover: *Ways of Nature: 18*, 2008

Michael Rosenfeld Gallery extends our gratitude to doctoral candidate Michelle DuBois for her outstanding essay. DuBois' fresh scholarship on artist Charles Seliger enhances our understanding of twentieth century American art.

ABOUT JOHN BURROGHS (1837-1921)

Born in 1837, the American naturalist and author John Burroughs grew up on his family's dairy farm in Roxbury, in the Catskill Mountains of New York. The seventh of ten children, Burroughs developed an early passion for nature that would persist throughout his life. As a child, he spent his time reading the books of John James Audubon in the library of West Point Academy, and he would also frequently slip out of class in order to study the plants and wildlife of the area. At seventeen, Burroughs left school to become a teacher. In his free time, he was an avid reader of Ralph Waldo Emerson, Henry David Thoreau, and Walt Whitman, and he began writing for the *Atlantic Monthly*. During the Civil War, Burroughs tried to enlist in the U.S. Army. Unsuccessful, in 1864, he moved to Washington, D.C. to work in the Treasury Department, which was understaffed due to the war. He and his wife lived in Washington for several years, during which he met and befriended Walt Whitman, who encouraged him to continue writing. Burroughs did, and in 1867, he published *Notes on Walt Whitman*, which was the first critical volume written on the poet. Burroughs followed this monograph with his first nature book, *Wake Robin* in 1871. Tired of city life and banking, Burroughs left Washington in 1874 and returned to rural New York, where he eventually dedicated himself to writing full-time. Over the course of his remaining decades, Burroughs published over twenty volumes of essays, including *Ways of Nature* (1905) and *Camping and Tramping with Roosevelt* (1906). Although he wrote on numerous subjects, he is best known for his nature essays, which not only celebrated the beauty of the natural world, but also made a powerful case for preserving it at a time of rapid and unprecedented industrial growth in the United States. A friend of early automotive industrialists Harvey Firestone and Henry Ford as well as such key members of the conservationist movement as Theodore Roosevelt and John Muir, Burroughs remains an important if less familiar figure in the history of environmentalism in the United States. He died in 1921, shortly before his eighty-fourth birthday, on train heading from California back to his cherished farms of upstate New York.